APARTMENT GREENERY

APARTMENT GREENERY

GROWING PLANTS IN UNPROMISING PLACES

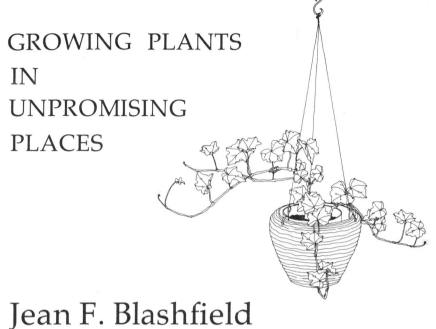

Jean F. Blashfield

Illustrations by Mary Purcell

LITTLE, BROWN AND COMPANY — BOSTON — TORONTO

FIRST EDITION

T 07/75

LIBRARY OF CONGRESS CATALOGING IN PUBLICATION DATA

Blashfield, Jean F
  Apartment greenery.

    1. House plants. I. Title.
SB419.B57   635.9'65   75-2310
ISBN 0-316-09954-6

Designed by Susan Windheim

*Published simultaneously in Canada
by Little, Brown & Company (Canada) Limited*

PRINTED IN THE UNITED STATES OF AMERICA

CONTENTS

*To my parents
who surrounded me with love
and green plants*

APARTMENT GREENERY

THE DREAM OF THE ROSE-COVERED COTTAGE—MODERN STYLE

WE ALL HAVE OUR OWN DREAM involving some future time when we will reside in a rose-covered (or perhaps vine-covered) cottage. It's a place where we can withdraw from the race and savor a feeling that we've earned our repose and that from now on only good things can happen.

Real cottages, however, are now few and far between. The streams running by them are probably polluted, and beautiful roses are more difficult to grow than the dream discloses.

Parts of the dream can be captured here and now, even in small places such as in-town apartments. One of the prime images given by the rose-covered cottage ideal is that of fresh and comfortable harmony with nature. Curiously enough, the effect is easier to achieve now than ever before. The warmth of apartments in winter and their comparative coolness in summer permit the growing of more plants indoors than has ever been possible. The color and fragrance of flowering plants, the various green tones and pleasing shapes of foliage plants, bring a softness to a room that relaxes frazzled nerves.

Plants are fascinating in their own right, beyond the effect they create on your decor. They react to you and the care you give them. Events unseen beneath the soil cause changes (good or bad) in the leaves and blossoms — and *you* make those events happen.

Until recently it was considered juvenile to talk of plants anthropomorphically, to describe their preferences, likes and dislikes, as if they were almost human: no longer. It's not that they have become like people — heaven knows there are enough of us around already. But we are coming to understand that plants react to their environment, and to us as part of that environment, in ways unimagined only a few years ago. Plants have certain "tastes" in music. They appear to grow better for people who talk to them than for people who just absent-mindedly tilt the watering can. They may react internally to tones of anger or sorrow in our voices, something that science fiction writers have been sure of for years.

A grape ivy friend of mine who accidentally was allowed to wilt did not perk up until a sincere apology was extended to it. Coincidence? Perhaps, perhaps not. If it works, don't question it (not, I fear, a very scientific attitude).

It used to be that the stereotypical thing for a woman to do when angry, frustrated, or upset was to go out and buy a hat, or for a man in the same state to tinker with his car. How much more calming it is to take advantage of the same mood to hunt for a new Swedish ivy or artillery plant, to repot those plants that have been begging for a new home, or to prune an *Impatiens* that has gone ape.

If you've never grown plants before, don't put off getting involved because it may be complicated. It's only as complex and time-consuming as you allow it to be. You can take as much pride in a healthy, twining philodendron as someone else may take in a display of rare orchids. Your plant is yours, and it's a valid part of the image of the embowered cottage if it brings new life and peace to your apartment.

Why wait? Dream no longer.

THE ECOLOGY OF YOUR APARTMENT

Do YOU EVER STAND by the window of a pet shop and yearn to take home an animal? Perhaps an independent-minded cat . . . a playful puppy . . . a stately turtle that will accept you as you.

But your lease says no small-print pets.

Think about plants.

Plants have personalities . . . or "phytumalities."

Some are gregarious and enjoy parties and good talk as much as you do.

Some are rather dignified; they respond to reason and clear thinking.

Some are playful and need discipline to be completely livable-with.

And others are solitary creatures who can absorb some neglect but not thoughtlessness.

Plants are friends who never, ever give advice. They are living roommates who don't have to be taken for walks on slushy, cold days. You won't even have to change a litter box.

Plants add life to small places. They cheer up apartments, soften austere offices, listen to your problems, thrive in response to your caring.

Like pets, however, not all plants can live comfortably in every situation. Apartments and other small places can rarely be all things to all plants. The environment offered is just not versatile enough. So you have to make choices — choices based on both the unchangeable conditions offered in your apartment and the different "phytumalities" of the plants you select.

With some analysis of the ecology of your apartment, you'll find that you can provide the proper conditions for many different plants.

Samuel Paul, a renowned apartment architect, has written: "The ultimate objective for the successful apartment project is balance. Not an innocuous balance that evokes little or no reaction, but a stimulating and dynamic balance that brings into proper perspective all the many complex requirements, controls and limitations inherent in the design of this type of building. A balance that displays imagination and creativeness and is tempered with reality."

The same holds true for the design of a dwelling shared by people and plants. An odd pot of greenery or two stuck around will probably survive. But for you and your home they will be part of an "innocuous balance." To achieve "stimulating and dynamic balance," you must use imagination and creativeness, tempered by the realities of the conditions your apartment provides and the basic requirements of the plants you select . . . as well as your own willingness to tend them.

Many plants massed around a window can be quite beautiful. But if that window is your only source of daylight, you are shutting yourself off from the outside world.

A single bushy plant with a lovely shape can look quite dramatic centered on a highly polished coffee table. But if that coffee table also serves as your dining table so that the plant needs to be moved regularly, the plant won't stay lovely very long.

A green divider between living room and dinette will bring oohs and aahs from visitors. But if they have to brush past the plants to sit down because the rooms are small, the visitors only help to destroy the object of their admiration.

Be realistic.

It would be great if you could just look at a plant, decide you like it, and take it home. You can if you'll be happy with plastic plants — some of which, admittedly, are quite well done these days. But if you want a living thing, one that grows and needs you, you must pick plants that fit the ecology of your apartment.

Look around. Consider. Evaluate the living conditions you offer. You can hedge and pretend, for example, that you have more light available than you actually do, but don't be surprised if your plants don't really like the pleasure of your company.

Be honest.

LIGHT FROM WINDOWS

I can't say that light is the one vital requirement for your plants, because light must be in balance with temperature and humidity. But without it, they starve — they can't produce their own food.

Some plants are more adaptable than others in their light requirements. There's no point in trying to grow cacti in a basement apartment where you have to turn on lamps to find lunch. That's true, too, for most flowering plants. But an aspidistra (don't laugh until you've actually tried one) might be quite happy there.

If you have a typical apartment, the windows probably all face the same direction. Consider yourself lucky if you have an end or corner apartment. More options are open to you in choosing your plants.

Your windows face north? You are limited to plants for north light and dark corners. They tend to be foliage plants with dark green leaves. They generally came from tropical lands where they lived at ground level beneath dark, sheltering forests.

Your windows face east or west? You get short periods of sunlight and have much more variety in selecting your plants than you would with north windows. You can regard spaces away from east or west windows as north light.

Your windows face south? You have a bright, sunny apartment. It gets very warm at noon and the light probably hurts your eyes. It will hurt many plants, too, unless you provide some shielding against the direct rays of the sun. Remember, as a child, trying to set fire to a piece of paper by holding glass between the sun and the paper? Direct sun can burn your plants. That's why greenhouses often have the south-facing windows painted. I'm not suggesting you paint your windows unless you're trying to break your lease, but do use a venetian blind to break up the sun's rays or hang a sheer curtain over the window to soften ("diffuse") the light for several hours around noon in summer. Neither of these precautions is necessary in winter when the sun is so far south that the rays are not so direct that they can do any harm. You can grow almost anything when you have south windows. Different places in your rooms duplicate north, east, and west light. Have fun.

What is outside your windows? The preceding comments hold true only if your windows are not obstructed. If you have south windows covered in summer by leafy trees, you already have a built-in filtration system. If you have north windows at right angles to a light-colored wing which reflects sun into your apartment, you have at least west light.

You get reflection inside your apartment, too. White walls — which seem to be standard nowadays — reflect a great deal of light. The reverse is also true. Victorian decor with dark walls and heavy drapes gives less light than window direction alone would indicate. Dark colors absorb light.

The far corners of your rooms may not be as uninhabitable as they first appear. Take a look during the brightest time of day. Do you get fairly strong shadows on the wall? If so, there are a number of plants you can grow. (As you go through "The Plant Guide," look for the ones that say "any" or "dark corners" under light requirements.) If the shadows have sharp, distinct edges, you actually have a great deal of light.

I have a grape ivy (Cissus rhombifolia) living quite happily twenty-two feet from north-facing windows. Admittedly, it lives on a stereo speaker and seems to derive much of its strength from Vivaldi and Telemann.

Remember your music in analyzing your apartment. The U.S. Department of Agriculture — yes, the government! — has determined that plants do better living with classical music than they do with hard rock. And they don't like violent arguments!

You have a skylight? Lucky you. Enjoy — just be sure to keep a sheer curtain over it if it gets direct sun in summer.

Your apartment faces north onto a deep airshaft, and still you yearn for greenery? Consider growing plants under electric lights (see "Artificial Light to Help the Sun").

You can, of course, buy a light-measuring device and evaluate the footcandles of light available where you want to place plants. But why not just think a little, experiment, and spend the money you save on a personable fern.

What this all comes down to in choosing plants is figuring out the most light you have available. You can use any plant requiring that light or less.

HUMIDITY

The humidity (or lack of it) will get you if you don't watch out! No matter how many plant books you read, you're always going to find references to the importance of humidity. Most plants, like people, need a fairly high level of moisture in the air to be comfortable. I remember when I lived in Chicago, where the air is dreadfully dry in winter. I would wake on cold mornings with a sore throat and my eyelids glued together. If dry air does that to people, imagine what it does to plants, which can't get up and wash their faces.

Dry air is a fact of life for apartment dwellers in

winter. No matter how humid it is outdoors, the artificial heat indoors is going to be much, much drier. In very few buildings is moisture added to the heat distributed through the building. In an average apartment in the North, the humidity in winter is about fifteen to thirty-five percent. Most plants need at least fifty percent, and ferns and African violets thrive in up to seventy percent (they love Washington, D.C., summers!).

Figure it this way. If you have a fixed amount of moisture in the air, the lower the temperature is, the higher will be the relative humidity of the air. So, if you don't want to (or can't) lower the temperature, you must add moisture to the air for the comfort of both you and your plants. (There's an added bonus for you if you manage to keep the humidity level fairly high: no painful static electricity shocks when you touch objects in winter.)

There are a number of possibilities open to you for raising the humidity of your apartment:

1. Consider getting a room humidifier. Doctors think that everyone would be healthier in winter with them. The machines gulp a great deal of water and need to be refilled often.

2. Put large pans of water on your radiators or other heating units. Be sure to keep them filled. Heat makes the water evaporate very quickly.

3. Place all plants requiring high humidity (most of them) on trays of pebbles. (This is not an alternative suggestion — this is necessary if you want healthy plants. See "Plant Needs and Wishes.")

4. The pleasantest alternative is to spray the leaves of each plant. Go around to each plant (daily in some cases), have a chat, and spray the leaves with room-temperature water. Carry a rag with you to wipe up the excess spray if the surfaces under the plants don't like to be watered.

5. Put plants in windows. Any moisture that's around condenses on cold glass. Windows are

cooler at night and that automatically raises the humidity. Don't let the leaves touch freezing glass, however.

6. Group plants together. As they transpire (give off moisture), the moisture becomes available for the other plants, raising the humidity level for the whole group.

7. Grow all your plants in terrariums (see "Terrariums").

8. Grow all your plants in the bathroom where the spray from the shower and sink add moisture to the air. Unfortunately, most apartment bathrooms don't have windows.

AIR

Air seems to be an obvious requirement. You know how uncomfortable you are in a stuffy, smoke-filled room. Most plants are less happy in stagnant air than people are, especially if the air is *dirty* and stagnant because the dirt settles on the leaves and prevents their breathing properly.

Air must be kept moving in order that fresh supplies of oxygen and carbon dioxide can reach the plants. Circulating air also slows the growth of fungi which might damage plants. Grimy air has less chance of clogging up breathing pores on leaves if it is kept moving. Think how often you have to wash gunk off your window sills and other woodwork. That muck, by-product of our modern cities, can settle on the plant. The dirtier your air is the more often you'll have to bathe your plants.

In spring and fall there's little chance of lack of fresh air being a problem unless you grew up with the belief that fresh air is bad for you. You probably keep windows open in your apartment. In winter, though, you may have to make a deliberate effort to keep air circulating. If your building has a central heating system with blowers in each apartment, the usual case with newish buildings, fresh air (about twenty-five percent) is brought in automatically. You have no problem.

If you have old-fashioned radiators, however, you'll have to try to open a window as often as possible, such as when you're out during the day. But make sure it doesn't blow directly on the plants. Drafts are more lethal than stagnant air. Plants catch cold. They get chilled and lose water from their leaves faster than it can be replaced. Use a room divider to block the drafts, or open a window in a different room.

Drafts don't have to be cold to be unhealthy. Which doors do you use most often? Keep plants away from them, as well as from windows that leak air. Older buildings tend to let little breezes in through ill-fitting windows. Light a candle and move it around your windows. If the flame jumps away from an unseen breeze, you've got the drafts. Keep plants away from them. Drafts reinforce other conditions: if the plant is cold, it gets chillier; if it's dry, it gets drier.

What about summer? Plants, like people, love air conditioning. Much scientific research went into this astounding conclusion.

It's not the coolness *per se* that plants like. It's the evenness of the temperature. A plant that doesn't have to adjust continually to changing conditions has more energy for other things — like growing.

Window air conditioners are not as helpful as central air conditioners. Window machines produce only massive cold drafts. Play with the candle again and find out where the centers of calm are in your rooms. Plan to keep the plants in those spots.

You've only one window and it contains an air conditioner? I'm afraid you'll have to limit yourself to "dark corner" plants far from the drafts.

TEMPERATURE

The international fuel shortage was somewhat uncomfortable for people, but plants were thriving. Plants don't mind heat by itself so much. It's the low humidity that goes along with high temperatures that does the damage.

The plants described in "The Plant Guide" have "warm" or "cool" temperatures listed for them. This is *nighttime* temperature, not daytime. In their native outdoors, all plants are subjected to temperature drops when the sun goes down. In fact, they need that drop. African violets are the only plants that like high nighttime temperatures. Most other flowering plants need quite a drop.

How much "drop" are we talking about? Those plants whose temperature requirement is described as "warm" should be at about sixty-five degrees at night. Those described as "cool" prefer a drop to about sixty degrees. "Coolish" means somewhere in between. (I am, of course, going on the assumption that your apartment's daytime temperature is between sixty-eight and seventy-two. If you and your plants became accustomed to between sixty-five and sixty-eight when the fuel shortage started, drop the night temperature five to ten degrees accordingly.)

If you're one of those people who wanders around naked with 3 A.M. insomnia, consider wearing a robe and turning down the thermostat before you go to bed, for the benefit of your plants.

You don't have a thermostat? The temperature is controlled by an unseen gnome who lives in the basement? Select the "warm" plants and keep them by windows. You'll probably have to stick to foliage plants. It is unlikely that you'll get good flowers without a temperature drop. Except, again, for African violets.

Find out the actual temperatures in your apartment. A thermostat records the temperature only at its location. It's probably warmer in a far corner, colder near the window. You'll need to stay up late one or two nights to get night temperature readings. Or, if you're really fascinated, get up before dawn for a reading. (It's not only darkest but also coldest before the dawn.) You can, however, avoid late nights and early days by getting a maximum-minimum thermometer. For later reference, the readings freeze at the high and low points reached by the thermometer. You don't have to be there.

So:

You know you want some living decoration.

You know what kind of sunlight you have to offer.

You know that you'll have to provide additional humidity unless you have a particular fondness for cacti; and that you'll have to regard pebble trays or moss-filled troughs as part of the visible decor of your apartment.

You know how dirty your air is and whether you'll have to provide additional circulation without drafts.

You know where you can put warmth-loving plants and where the cool ones would prefer to be.

Make your way through "The Plant Guide." Visit garden shops. Find the plants you like. If you pick plants that fit your conditions and decor but don't really like them, neither you nor the plants will be happy. Most plants aren't really all that fond of indoor living; they just tolerate it. Don't make them just tolerate you, too.

Be friendly!

MATERIALS YOU WILL NEED

THE ABSOLUTE NECESSITIES for taking care of apartment plants are few:

> an apartment
> plants
> pots
> soil
> tray
> pebbles
> sprayer
> watering can
> fertilizer and measuring spoon
> a willingness to get your hands dirty

Beyond that list, there are some common items
that simplify the occasional work to be done, such
as a spoon for handling soil, and others that are
needed only if you elect to grow certain plants; for
example, those that require sand or perlite in their
soil.

Basically, though, unless you go pot-buying-
happy, you should be able to keep everything in a
reasonably sized box that will fit in a kitchen
cupboard.

POTS

A pot to hold a plant can be any container that will
hold soil and has enough room for the roots of the

plant. However, I do not believe that there is such a thing as a healthy, easy-to-care-for plant in a pot without a drainage hole in the bottom; it's just too easy to overwater a plant in a holeless pot (creating infinite problems), or to underwater because of fear of overwatering.

Ergo, I suggest you eschew ceramic donkeys, supine hollow nudes, or trumpeting white elephants. Give them to a white elephant sale or grow only plants that will live in water (see "Plants with Something Extra").

There are basically three kinds of useful pots, which come in all sizes, from two-inch (diameter across the top) to eight-inch and more.

Clay pots are the familiar, unglazed, red-rust ones that have been used for generations. They are always that color because clay when baked always turns that color. Some people don't like it. I do: when planted, such pots tell me "life is here."

Clay pots have advantages and disadvantages, and you must make your choice according to how they weigh with you:

1. They weigh with you! They are heavy, especially when filled with damp soil and pebbles. This, of course, is an advantage with top-heavy plants.

2. They break if dropped, but then, so might you. Broken pots give you a supply of crocking material (pot bits) for use over the drainage holes in whole pots.

3. They are cold-blooded, changing temperature with the air temperature — but it's unlikely that your apartment temperature changes enough for that to matter.

4. They allow water to evaporate through the sides: a disadvantage if you're trying to keep the soil moist, an advantage in that the evaporated moisture raises the humidity around the plant. Conversely, they let air in, which almost all roots need. However, water also evaporates through the

bottom of the saucers and may condense on the surface below. Don't use clay saucers directly on wooden tabletops.

5. They tend to accumulate salts from water and fertilizer on their sides. But this residue is easy to scrub off. If your pots turn white from salts quickly, cut down on the amount of fertilizer you are using.

6. They are becoming harder and harder to find in this age of plastic.

For me, the search is worth it. The comforts of less dangerous watering, plus the fact that my cats can't knock the pots over easily (though when they do, the pots shatter), make clay pots my choice for all plants except African violets and the plants that live under lights.

Plastic pots are beneficial for plants under artificial lights just because they aren't porous and thus don't lose water through the sides. They don't heat up under the lights, and they are easy to keep clean. The fact that water doesn't go through them, however, means that air doesn't either. So your plants in plastic pots need the top layer of their soil aerated a bit occasionally. Loosen it gently all over with a fork. Don't gouge down into the roots. Water less and fertilize a great deal less in plastic pots than in clay pots.

To my mind, one of the major problems with plastic pots is that I have yet to see one in a decent color. They are often hospital green; and orange, white, and disgustingly vivid silver ones are becoming ubiquitous.

Plastic pots may come sealed on the bottom, with straight or circular indentations in the flat surface. Use a sharp tool to punch out the indented part, making drainage holes. Be sure to pick pots with good-sized holes and use a layer of pebbles in the bottom.

Many plastic pots in all shapes come with attachable saucers and watering wicks. When planting, you run the wick from the soil base to the saucer below. In theory, you add water to the saucer and it is drawn by capillarity up the wick as the soil dries on top. You may be lucky and find wicks useful for constant-moisture-loving plants. However, it's easy to develop a horrid gray scum of mold on top of the soil. I don't like the feeling of being less in control of the water situation than when I do the watering myself.

A third type of pot is beginning to be seen across the land — Styrofoam. These pots are exceedingly light in weight, making it, I would think, essential that you use sand and pebbles in the soil rather than perlite, so that they won't tip easily. The ones I've seen — and I haven't used any yet — are an attempt to match the same rust color of clay pots. I'm told they let air in but not water out. They should be especially useful for hanging plants when you're not sure how much weight your walls can bear. An additional feature is that stems dangling over the side aren't continually gnawed at by a hard, bruising edge. The very softness of the Styrofoam, however, means that every scratch and knock leaves a scar forever.

What about jardinieres, decorative pots into which you put the utilitarian pot? Fine, go ahead and use them if you want. Just follow three rules. One, put pebbles in the bottom to take the runoff from watering, and look down in there after watering to be sure not too much water has accumulated. Two, make sure there's at least an inch of air space all around the inner pot, more if the jardiniere is nonbreathing plastic. Three, don't let the jardiniere be deeper than the pot: the plants look funny, and they don't like being laughed at. If necessary, build up the inner pot with pebbles.

SOIL

Standard potting soil is the commercial mixture available in grocery stores, dime stores, almost anywhere, and it is usually just labeled "potting soil."

The bags (five pounds, ten pounds, etc.) may say "for philodendrons and other house plants." Potting soil is a basic mixture of decaying vegetable material (peat), sand, and (usually) vermiculite, combined in the proper proportions needed by most plants. It has been sterilized to kill bacteria, weed seeds, and fungi. The formulas used were derived from a great deal of research by the government and university horticultural departments. The brands are all somewhat different, but they all work well for most apartment plants.

Potting soil contains a great deal of nutrient, so your plants should not need to be additionally fertilized for eight months or more even if the soil you buy comes with a gift supply of fertilizer enclosed, as Baccto does. However, if you add chopped peat moss, sand, or other extra ingredients, you will need to feed the plants sooner.

Some plants require a little bit of extra material mixed with the potting soil. More sand increases the drainage; more chopped peat increases the water-holding capacity of the soil.

As you'll see from the shelves at the store, there are other soil varieties available that have their uses. African violet mix is richer in the water-holding vegetation than standard soil. African violets, episcias, and rex begonias are some plants that like it. Your ferns should do well in it, too. Whenever "The Plant Guide" says "add chopped peat to standard potting soil," you can use African violet mix if you have it on hand.

Cactus soil is very sandy, so there's no chance of wet soil compacting to plant tissues that already hold a great deal of water, making them rot. Cacti and other succulent plants do well in this special mix. You can, however, mix sand and pebbles with standard potting soil to create cactus soil.

Soilless "soils" are often used for bromeliads, *Asplenium*, and a few other plants. They generally consist of broken-up bark or tough plant fiber, leaf mold, and sand. Rather than invest in them, you can create your own by mixing a little potting soil with lots of sand and peat moss.

DRAINAGE MATERIALS

The one big physical effort you will need to make, unless you trot home with overlarge plants, is bringing home a supply of pebbles. Most apartment plants are humidity lovers that need to live on a tray filled with pebbles in water. Also, a layer of pebbles in the bottom of most pots will help negate the serious effects of overwatering by allowing water to drain below the soil and roots. You can use coarse perlite for this purpose instead of pebbles. It's a lot lighter in weight, however, which means that heavy pots can easily tilt when placed on a layer of perlite in trays.

Perlite is particles of expanded volcanic rock which absorb and hold water, an advantage for soil that needs to be kept moist. It also allows air to get into the soil and it is very lightweight — which simplifies the task of carrying it home. However, it is white and stands out in a soil mixture. It can be used instead of sand for mixing with soil that must drain quickly, or it can be used alone as a layer beneath soil for the same purpose.

Vermiculite is also an exploded mineral, mica. It's incredibly lightweight and absorbs a great deal of water. It makes soil porous. It, however, slowly condenses from the weight of the soil, losing its water-retention feature. It doesn't show in the soil as glaringly as perlite does. Vermiculite and perlite are both good materials for use in rooting cuttings.

The sand used in gardening is not the kind found in sand boxes. Gardening sand is often called sharp sand or builder's sand. The grains of sand are sharp-edged and water does not adhere to them. This aids the drainage of water through the soil. Don't get sand from an ocean beach; the salt content is difficult to wash away.

Sand is used mixed with soil to increase drainage and to prevent the soil from compacting into a solid mass. It is also useful with chopped peat to root cuttings. You can make your own choice among perlite, vermiculite, and sand-peat for rooting — usually depending on what you have on hand. You shouldn't have to keep more than a small bag of sand available unless you plan to create a cactus-bearing desert in your apartment.

You can use perlite instead of sand, but perlite has the disadvantage of being so light that tall, heavy plants may not stand up in soil mixed with much perlite.

PEAT MOSS

Peat moss is partially decayed sphagnum moss, a primitive plant that grows in moist places, turns lakes into bogs, and eventually turns into the fuel called peat. Chopped peat moss is often added to soil both to give it a rougher consistency and to increase its moisture-holding capability. It also adds a slight acidity to the soil, which some plants like. The moss, easily available in garden shops in small quantities, must be soaked in water for a few minutes before it's mixed with soil, or it will never absorb water.

Because it does absorb water — assuming you've soaked it well — sand or perlite also needs to be added to soil containing extra peat moss so that water that is not absorbed can drain out and air can reach the plant roots.

If you have a group of plants in pots resting on pebbles in a tall-sided planter (as opposed to just on a pebble tray), you can use peat moss strands (not chopped peat) around the pots to hold moisture. Humidity is increased and evaporation from the pots is slowed. Don't do this if the planter is in dim light because the plants can't handle so much moisture.

TRAY

A plastic, fiberglass, or rustproof metal tray two or three inches deep is an absolute necessity for many apartment plants, especially in winter. Almost fill the tray with pebbles or perlite, add water to within an inch of the top of the pebble layer, and you have an automatic humidifier for plants standing on the pebbles. Excess water from overwatering can run away to where it won't harm roots: just be sure to water your plants first, wait half an hour or so for water to run out, then add water to the tray if needed. If you fill the tray and then water your plants, the excess that drains out may be enough to leave the pots sitting in water, causing problems.

Such trays also save you the cost of saucers for all your pots. Deep baking pans will do, if you like the look of metal. I use plastic Kitchenmaid drawer dividers for small plants. They cost, if I remember correctly, seventy-nine cents each. With large plants, just fill the pot's saucer itself with pebbles to catch the drainage.

Be sure to wash the tray and its pebble contents every few months. They collect dust and can breed pests.

WATERING CAN

You can pour water out of anything, of course. But some plants form too tight a mass of leaves over the top of the pot to let you get, say, a cup near the soil. Other plants object vehemently and brown-spottedly to getting their leaves wet. And, of course, you may have plants in baskets hanging above your head. It's safest all around to buy a watering can with a long spout. Be sure it is large enough to let you put a spoon in it to stir fertilizer solution.

FERTILIZER

See "Plant Needs and Wishes."

SPRAYER OR MISTER

There are many kinds of sprayers (a mister is just a male chauvinist sprayer) on the market today — from bulb types to miniature spray guns, as well as cute brass ones that look nice with early Americana but which, frankly, almost always drip. I've got just three recommendations for selecting it. One, be sure it gives a fine mist. Two, be sure the water container holds at least a cup of water so that what you don't use in humidifying your plants one time is available at room temperature the next time you use it. Three, pick one you like and are comfortable using — you'll use your sprayer (at least you should!) more than any other piece of equipment. If there's something about it that makes you put off using it, regard it as a bad investment and find one that makes you delight in spraying your plants regularly.

SPOONS

You might as well set aside one sturdy spoon, preferably a table spoon with a narrow handle, mentally or actually labeling it "I belong to the plants." You'll need it for spooning soil from bag to pot, poking through the hole in the bottom of a pot when a plant in need of transplanting is reluctant to leave its familiar home, stirring fertilizer solution, tamping down soil, and so on. Select one, cherish it, and pass it through to future generations as "grandperson's plant spoon."

You'll also need measuring spoons for measuring fertilizer. The smaller the spoon, the safer for your plants. Don't be tempted to measure out half a teaspoon of fertilizer by guessing where the middle of a teaspoon measure is.

INSECTICIDE

See "When Your Green Thumb Turns Plants Brown."

KNIFE

Dig into your kitchen utensil drawer for a sharp but sturdy knife that you can dedicate to your plants. You'll need it for pruning stems too hard to pinch and for trimming roots when transplanting. Keep it clean and at the ready. A meat-greasy dull

Materials You Will Need 23

blade hiding behind your garlic press won't help much when you're in a hurry.

STAKES AND STRING

Many plants reach heights undreamed of when you bought them. Their tall stems may need support. Vines need a place to climb. You will need plant stakes to take care of these situations, and string or special plant tapes to tie the plant stem to the stake.

A plant stake may be a simple, green, bamboo pole for plants that just need a bit of support. Tie the stem to the stake just tight enough to hold the stem upright without damaging it. Fancier stakes on which climbing plants can gain handholds are squared-off poles called "tree ferns." They absorb and hold moisture from the spraying of plants. A third type, often seen with philodendrons, is a piece of cedar log with the bark still covering one rounded side.

You can, of course, invent your own plant stakes. Just don't use a coat hanger or other metal that will rust, and be sure it's very clean.

COMBINATION HYGROMETER– THERMOMETER

This extra little goody is by no means vital, but–it saves a lot of wear and tear on your nerves and doesn't cost much. A hygrometer is a device to measure moisture in the air. Taylor's Humidiguide is an inexpensive, square, plastic one which gives readings of approximate temperature and relative humidity. Place it among your plants but not on the pebble tray. Watch the readings change from morning to afternoon, from bright days to rainy days. In winter, try to keep the humidity reading above fifty percent for the health of your plants.

Don't invest in too many gadgets for your plants until you discover a real need that can be filled by them. Use the money instead for new plants. Keep all the materials you do use with your plants absolutely clean, and your new friends should be around for a long time.

HOW TO GET POTTED

STEP ONE: spread out newspapers.

I hate to be obvious, but potting plants is messy work. You spend, it seems, 107 percent of your life keeping your apartment clean and then here you are, deliberately playing about in dirt. At least you can keep the mess in one place, on paper that can be rolled up and thrown away. (Note: pebbles won't go down a garbage disposal.)

You find a new plant you like and bring it home to your apartment. It looks top-heavy and pot-bound in the little plastic pot it came in, so you move it right away into a larger, more attractive pot, right? Wrong!

It has been doing all right for a while in the small pot it's in now, or you wouldn't have picked it as a healthy plant. Let it get used to its new surroundings for a few days. If you add the trauma of re-potting into a larger pot to that of a move from greenhouse to apartment, you may shock a delicate plant beyond mending.

Water the plant the day before you plan to repot it. The soil will be easy to handle when not too wet or too dry. Select and prepare the new pot (one size larger than the pot the plant came in) ahead of time so you don't have to abandon the plant with roots dangling in midair while you scurry around. If you're using a new clay pot, it, too, should be watered the day before planting. Clay pots, in spite of their heavy, solid feel, are porous; water evaporates through the sides constantly. So if you start with the pot soaked in water, the water you use when repotting won't disappear immediately into the clay. If you use an old pot, you have washed it thoroughly long before, back when you removed the plant it contained. (That's not a question, it's a statement.) Soak an old pot overnight, too.

Put a piece of broken pot (called crock) over the hole in the bottom, curved side up. Excess water will be able to escape but soil won't. If the plant guide instructions call for very good drainage, add a shallow layer of pebbles or perlite over the crock (use a deeper layer in a plastic pot). Even if the instructions don't specifically call for good drainage, it's probably wise to put a pebble layer in every pot.

Add a little soil or soil mixture to the pot. Press it down firmly, leaving a hole deep enough to take the old soil ball. You'll want about half an inch of watering space left at the top of a small pot, about an inch in a larger pot.

Remove the plant from the old pot by turning the plant upside down with your hand cupped over the mouth of the pot, plant stem between your fingers. Knock the pot sharply against the edge of a sink or counter, but not so hard that the pot breaks. The soil should separate cleanly without your having to pull on the plant — why shake it up more than necessary? If it doesn't loosen, give it an encouraging push with a spoon handle or pencil pushing on the crock through the hole in the bottom.

Stand the plant in its soil ball in the new pot, positioned as you want it. If it was crooked before, straighten it now. If the watering space at the top is not right, add or remove soil from the bottom of the pot (you must not plan to add soil to the top: plants don't like the soil level on their stems changed). Pour fresh soil around the outside of the soil ball, tamping it down firmly all around with a spoon, dowel, or fingers. The new soil must be as firm as the old or the roots will shy away from the different texture and not take advantage of the new growing space. Thump the bottom of the pot firmly on a flat surface. Loose soil will pack down, eliminating air pockets.

Water the freshly potted plant completely. Let water run through and out. You may use a weak fertilizer solution to give the plant energy to overcome shock and root damage; follow the directions on the fertilizer container. Don't return a sun-loving plant to direct sun right away; keep it in dimmer light for ten days or so while it catches its breath.

Don't water again until the soil is drying. Transplanted roots need a chance to grow sturdily before they are again faced with the danger of overwatering.

When potting a rooted cutting, you won't have a soil ball to deal with if you rooted it in water or sand. Ready your materials ahead of time. (You'll need tiny pots to start with.) Put a piece of crock over the hole, pour in soil to the top, then tap it gently down. Dig a hole in the center with your finger or a stick. Stand the cutting in the hole, with the roots spread out, and press soil around it. If you've been rooting the cutting for some time and it has developed a great deal of root, hold the plant in an almost empty pot and dribble soil around it, firming it to the roots.

THE ANNUAL CHECKUP

If you're doing your job of plant tending well, any healthy plant gradually outgrows the pot it is in and must be moved into a larger pot. If not transplanted, plants get pot-bound, which means that the roots have grown so much they turn in on themselves and are unable to take advantage of either the minerals or the water in the soil. There is soon too much root for the soil in the pot. Some plants, of course, do best when they are pot-bound — energy goes, for example, into blossoming instead of root growth. Also, large plants should be kept somewhat pot-bound in order to slow their growth.

Into the lives of most plants, however, comes a time when they should be given a roomier pot. If you see roots growing out the drainage hole and the plant shouldn't be pot-bound, transfer it right away into a larger pot. Don't put repotting on a far-future agenda. The plant needs help now.

For small plants, prepare a fresh pot, one inch larger than the old one. Very large plants can go into a pot two inches larger, so there is a full inch of new space all around. Knock the plant out of the old pot, handling the dangling, exposed roots carefully. Gently loosen tangled roots so they can breathe freely. You may have to work bits of crock or pebbles out from among the roots. Carefully check the condition of the roots as described below. If they are healthy, go ahead and position the plant in the pot as for first-time potting.

If you're really faithful about anticipating your plants' needs, you will knock them out of their pots at least once a year to check on the condition of the roots. The overgrown roots may not have worked their way through the drainage hole to visibility but they may still need help.

When you remove a plant from its pot, the soil should come out in a pot-shaped lump. Some roots will be visible. Take a good look at them. If the roots are healthy, they are firm and appear white or yellowish. There should be a fuzzy aura about the tips created by very fine root hairs, which are the vital parts that absorb water. If you've been letting the roots sit in soggy water, they will appear brown or black and will be squishy. They are rotting.

Carefully cut away rotted roots with a sharp

knife, going down into the good root material. Repot the plant in fresh soil, with good drainage under it, using a smaller pot than before if you have had to cut away much. From then on, resolve to be more conservative when wielding the watering can.

You will also need to cut away a proportionate amount of leaves when you cut the roots. Otherwise, the weak roots can't keep up with the top and the whole plant may fail (see "Plant Needs and Wishes").

If, on inspection, the mushiness of the roots appears to extend deep into the heart of the root ball, the best place to pot the plant is in the trash can. If sentiment keeps you from that drastic action and the plant will root from slips, take cuttings of the leaves or stems. But remember, you'll be starting new plants from less than vigorous cuttings — chancy at best.

Never anticipate a need for a bigger pot than the plant can handle. Use too big a pot and you'll get a plant with long, scraggly roots and a puny top. Which part looks most attractive? If you like the appearance of roots, consider water-growing plants (see "Plants with Something Extra").

Very large plants don't need the encouragement of new growing space, nor is it likely that you can repot them without damage to both them and you. Instead, you can cheer them up with a new hat, called top dressing. Carefully remove a couple of inches of the old soil at the top of the pot. Work as carefully as an archaeologist on a dig so that you never chip or otherwise endanger a root. Refill the space with new soil, making sure it tamps to exactly the same level on the plant stem as before. Give the plant a hearty meal of fertilizer and be glad that the real repotting has been put off for another year.

Repotting is a nuisance, but it's as necessary a step as replacing a child's outgrown clothes. The simplest way is to gather all but your largest plants about you once each spring and tackle them all at once. Have pleasant music going. Tell the plants how much happier they'll be in their new homes with refreshing supplies of nice soil. Then get to work.

THE PLANT GUIDE

WHAT IS AN APARTMENT OR OFFICE PLANT? It's a house plant with a carefree attitude toward life — like yours, I hope.

The plants described and illustrated here are those that you can tend with limited time and space. They don't go through dreary rest periods before bursting into bloom. They don't require esoteric materials that clog up your cupboards. They aren't tubers, which need to just sit for a couple of months every year. They don't have to spend the summer in your nonexistent garden. They don't include the familiar bulb plants such as crocus and amaryllis. I suggest you buy those when you see them on the market in late winter. Follow the directions that come with them, enjoy the blossoms, then throw away the bulbs.

What do these plants do? They generally stay green (or purple, or red, or even white) all year long. They bloom on and off with no extraordinary effort on your part. They look good even when they're not blooming. They include enough variety to fill most of your plant needs or fit the type of environment you can provide. They make you feel creative by throwing out new leaves when you least expect them. They listen uncomplainingly to the gruesome story of your day.

Don't worry at this point about the meaning of some of the instructions; you'll understand them when you've read the rest of the book. Concentrate on choosing those plants that fit the ecology of your apartment as you've determined it to be.

The plants in this chapter are listed by their botanical names because common names are apt to be confusing. Mother of thousands, for example, can be one of two quite different plants described: *Tolmiea menziesii* (also called the piggyback plant) or *Saxifraga sarmentosa* (also called strawberry geranium, although it's neither a strawberry nor a geranium).

When I was a child I heard someone talking about *Cotoneaster horizontalis* (it's an outdoor shrub). The name delighted me because it tumbled impressively off the tongue, but I found it difficult to work into conversations. Its later effect was to keep me from panicking at the sight of a Latin name. Don't be afraid of botanical names. Pronounce them just as they look, taking a guess when there are lots of vowels together.

To help you find a plant that interests you if you've heard of it only under a common name, use the index.

At the end of each plant discussion in this chapter are words indicating some characteristics of the plant or its care that will help you in selecting your plants. A handy reference chart of this information for all the plants appears at the end of the book. These descriptive words have the following meanings:

FOLIAGE — the plant is grown primarily for its evergreen leaves. Some foliage plants may produce small flowers but they are not showy enough or long-lasting enough to be important. Others have lovely flowers at long intervals and so are called both foliage and flowering.

FLOWERING — the plant is grown primarily for its flowers. Most of the flowering plants included

FINDING WHAT YOU'RE LOOKING FOR

here, however, are still attractive when they are not blooming. Apartments generally don't have room for an "ugly corner" where plants can be hidden away when they're dormant and dead-looking.

EASY — just that. If you provide even minimal care, the plant will cooperate — within reason, of course.

TERRARIUM — a plant that is small enough, at least as a young thing that can leave its mother, to fit into a terrarium. It doesn't grow so rapidly that you must remove it in just a few weeks.

OFFICE — a plant that generally thrives under fluorescent office lights, although it would appreciate indirect light sometimes. It doesn't require lots of tender loving care. Just be sure that everyone in the office doesn't decide separately to water the plant at the same time; even in an office, plants give up under too much watering. Of course, almost any plant will grow in an office if you care for it as you would at home and it doesn't freeze or sit in total darkness on long weekends (see "Plastic Plants Make Plastic Ideas").

WATER — a plant that can be grown in water instead of soil (see "Plants with Something Extra").

HANGING AND/OR CLIMBING — a plant that can be displayed in a special way (see "Plants with Something Extra").

Remember that "warm" means a night temperature of about sixty-five degrees. "Cool" means a night temperature of sixty or lower. "Coolish" is in between.

ADIANTUM (Maidenhair fern)

LIGHT — preferably east or west but will tolerate north if it can have a brighter holiday occasionally. However, don't move it too often; ferns like to stay in familiar surrounds.

TEMPERATURE — quite tolerant but would prefer coolish.

Adiantum tererum

HUMIDITY — lots; keep it on a pebble tray and spray the leaves daily.

WATERING — keep the soil quite moist but not soggy. Use less water if you have the plant in north light.

FEEDING — once a month.

SOIL — add chopped peat moss to the soil to keep it light. All ferns need good drainage so that water doesn't sit around the roots.

PROPAGATION — divide the root clump when re-potting.

The maidenhairs are a little more difficult to keep happy than other ferns are. Some writers say you shouldn't even try them unless you have a green-house, but others have good luck. So, if you're feeling lucky and want a soft-looking, rather friendly plant, try a maidenhair. If you're fond of ginkgo trees (ancient trees which should have been extinct by now but they seem to thrive in polluted cities), you'll like the maidenhairs. Ginkgoes are often called maidenhair trees because of the resemblance of their leaves to the fern leaflets.

The name *Adiantum* means "dry." The leaflets are said to shed water, but that doesn't mean you dare let the plant get dry. It needs lots of moisture.

Don't panic if your plant suddenly loses all its leaves, leaving the black, wirelike stems bare. It's not necessarily dead, it just needs a rest. Cut it back and feed it when it starts growing again.

If you grow *Adiantum* in a terrarium, be warned that you'll need to reach it to prune dead fronds. Use a large-mouthed container.

FOLIAGE; TERRARIUM

AECHMEA   (Living vase plant)

LIGHT — any except extremes. Some sun, how-ever, guarantees that the leaf color will stay bright.

Aechmea fasciata

TEMPERATURE — warm but can stand cool.

HUMIDITY — lots. Keep the "vase" — the central cup formed by the tubular cluster of leaves — filled with water which has sat for a day so that chlorine can escape. Spray the whole plant daily.

WATERING — let the soil get almost dry between waterings, but be sure to keep the vase filled.

FEEDING — once a month.

SOIL — add a good deal of sand and chopped peat moss to a little standard potting soil, or, if you have it, use a soilless orchid mixture. Be sure the pot drains well.

PROPAGATION — separate the maturing offsets (small plants that grow around the base) and plant them in peat moss. They should be at least four to six inches tall before they are separated. The mother plant will eventually wither.

Aechmea and its close relative *Billbergia* (some botanists put them in the same genus) are bromeliads, the most common examples of which are pineapple and Spanish moss. They are air-living plants — they don't really need soil to survive. They can perch on tree limbs or rest blandly on the exposed roots of a jungle tree, lying in wait to chop up the legs of passersby with their tooth-edged leaves. (Spanish moss is a bit of the family black sheep in this respect.)

Bromeliads can live without soil because water is taken in primarily through the leaves, with the roots doing little more than anchoring the plant. Nutrition — believe it or not — comes from dust. You can use a shallow pot for an *Aechmea*, or, for a special effect, fill a notch in a striking piece of driftwood with moss, insert the roots and tie the plant into an attractive position. The tie can be removed when the plant anchors itself.

Aechmeas grow to be one to two feet tall. The popular hybrid "Foster's Favorite" has a red flower spike most often appearing in winter. The leaves are wine-colored (brighter red in brighter light) on the back. *Aechmea fasciata* (often called the "urn plant" for its shape) has silver-cream, striped leaves and blue flowers in pink modified leaves called bracts, usually in spring. *Aechmea racinae* is green-leaved with red and yellow flowers. The flowers on all of them may last several months.

A seemingly mad suggestion, but it works. if your bromeliads aren't inclined to bloom, enclose them in a plastic bag with a ripe apple. It's not magic. After three or four weeks, the ethylene gas given off by the apple encourages blossoming. Don't try it with other plants, though; it will destroy the flower buds of more particular plants.

FOLIAGE; FLOWERING; TERRARIUM WHEN SMALL

AGLAONEMA   (Chinese evergreen)

LIGHT — any except bright sun.

TEMPERATURE — any.

HUMIDITY — any, but do spray occasionally.

WATERING — keep the soil moist. Let it dry before rewatering when the plant is not actively growing.

FEEDING — once a month.

SOIL — standard potting soil.

PROPAGATION — root stem cuttings.

Aglaonema commutatum

This colorful plant is so easy to care for and it tolerates people so well that it is a standard suggestion in children's books on growing plants indoors. Its large, pointed leaves are basically dark green, but several varieties are marbled or striped with gray-green or cream. When the plant has matured, it can have a bloom that looks like a green-tinged calla lily, which belongs to the same family.

Chinese evergreen is from Southeast Asia and nearby islands — monsoon country. Its vowel-filled Latin name means "bright thread."

Aglaonema grows easily in water; give it a deep container because the stems of the plain-colored plant can grow two or three feet long. The mottled ones tend to be shorter.

FOLIAGE; EASY; TERRARIUM; OFFICE; WATER

ANTHURIUM   (Flamingo flower, Tailflower)

LIGHT — east, west, or shaded south.

TEMPERATURE — warm.

HUMIDITY — keep quite high; spray daily.

WATERING — keep the soil very moist, almost wet.

FEEDING — every two weeks; use a weak fertilizer solution.

SOIL — add chopped peat to standard potting soil; be sure the pot drains well so that the leaves won't turn brown, a signal that the plant is in danger of rotting.

PROPAGATION — divide the root clump.

Anthurium scherzerianum

I spent years calling my spathiphyllum a white anthurium. I blushed when I found out it wasn't, and lately I've learned I'm not alone. Many people, including some botanists, say they belong in the same genus. They, as well as *Aglaonema* and others, are members of the arum family, distinguished by small, white flowers within colorful bracts, which are often thought to be the flowers.

The anthurium's bracts are vivid, waxy red, almost flat. They are often used as color accents in bouquets. The bracts, which last for weeks, also occur in white and pink.

The plant is also called flamingo flower. Its other common name, tailflower, is the translation of its Latin name. It blooms best in the fall, but it will blossom year round if you keep the plant warm. The temperature shouldn't be allowed to drop below sixty-five degrees. The requirements of high temperature and high humidity make *Anthurium* a demanding plant, but the results, whether you get flowers or just the dark, leathery foliage, are worth it.

FOLIAGE; FLOWERING; TERRARIUM

ARAUCARIA EXCELSA   (Norfolk Island pine)

LIGHT — north, east, or west. Shade a south window if you must use one.

TEMPERATURE — coolish.

HUMIDITY — fairly tolerant of dry apartment air in winter, but it's happier with extra moisture. Use a pebble tray or mossy trough.

WATERING — keep the soil moist.

FEEDING — two or three times a year. If the tree is quite large, don't feed more than once a year.

SOIL — standard potting soil.

PROPAGATION — you really shouldn't need to propagate it, and none of the methods is very reliable. But if you really want to try, cut several inches off the growing tip of the central trunk and root it. Don't try it, however, if your parent plant is quite young, because the top will lose its pretty shape. You can also root growing tips of side branches, but these don't yield trees of the classic shape.

Araucaria excelsa

This is a tree! I have a five-foot-tall one named Livingstone in my living room. Talk about conversation pieces!

The Norfolk Island pine is a relative of the delightful monkey puzzle tree. They are not true pines but evergreens from the Southern Hemisphere. The monkey puzzle tree was first discovered in Arauco, a province of Chile; hence the name.

The ubiquitous Captain Cook discovered Norfolk Island while crossing the South Pacific on his voyage around the world. He took home samples of the beautiful, symmetrical trees that covered the island. They quickly became popular house plants. On Norfolk Island, the pines grow to be two hundred feet tall — but don't let that put you off. You won't have to cut a hole in your ceiling unless you want to antagonize your upstairs neighbor. Just keep the tree pot-bound after it nears the height you like.

A real plus for the Norfolk Island pines: they make wonderful living Christmas trees. Be sure to use only the tiny lights so the needles won't scorch, keep humidity high, and don't weigh the branches down with heavy ornaments.

FOLIAGE

ASPARAGUS PLUMOSUS   (Asparagus fern)

ASPARAGUS SPRENGERI   (Emerald feather)

LIGHT — east or west; north may be acceptable.

TEMPERATURE — cool; even likes cold nights in winter.

HUMIDITY — some; keep on pebble tray. Doesn't need as high a humidity level as the real ferns do, but the warmer your apartment, the more moisture it will need.

WATERING — let the soil dry before watering again thoroughly.

FEEDING — every two or three weeks, especially when actively growing.

SOIL — mix peat moss with standard potting soil. Be sure the pot has good drainage.

PROPAGATION — divide the root clump or, if you're not impatient, plant seeds. *Asparagus plumosus* can be difficult to propagate; consider buying new plants.

Asparagus plumosus

The asparagus ferns are not real ferns; they are flowering plants of the lily family. But don't expect to be charmed by the flowers, which are almost invisible. Asparagus ferns are in the same genus as the vegetable, and if you've ever seen

Asparagus sprengeri

wild edible asparagus, you'll recognize the orna-
mental asparagus ferns right away. They give a
filmy, evanescent effect because the leaves are delicate "needles" instead of being broad and flat.

Emerald feather (*A. sprengeri*) is bright green
with half- or three-quarter-inch needle-shaped
leaves growing in clusters on long stems that arc
outward. Unlike needles, however, the leaves are
soft and delicate. They turn yellow if they don't
get enough light. Remove old stems to encourage
fresh, full growth. Red berries may appear in the
winter.

Asparagus plumosus, the type most often called
asparagus fern, or lace fern, is the delicate greenery
florists arrange with cut roses or as backing on a
corsage. When cut, it lasts without water for a
long while, but don't neglect your potted plants.
They do need water even though they originated
in the dry parts of South Africa.

Both emerald feather and asparagus fern should
be pinched back so that they keep a shapely look.
Emerald feather, however, is by nature a shaggier
plant than the asparagus fern. If you prefer asparagus fern to grow tall instead of hanging, add a

support to the pot. Emerald feather will climb around twine attached to a solid surface at top and bottom, making it useful as a room divider.

FOLIAGE; TERRARIUM; HANGING OR CLIMBING

ASPIDISTRA ELATIOR   (Cast-iron plant)

LIGHT — any. It's even happy in dark corners.

TEMPERATURE — any, but try to keep it out of extremes.

HUMIDITY — tolerant, but, like most plants, it prefers more rather than less. Spray the leaves when you think of it (which should be every time you have your sprayer out).

WATERING — keep the soil slightly damp but, again, it's pretty tolerant.

FEEDING — once a month.

SOIL — standard potting soil.

PROPAGATION — divide the root clump.

I'm thinking of renaming *Aspidistra* the "any" plant because it takes just about anything you want to throw at it — except total neglect and hatred. It has long been known as the cast-iron plant because of the toughness of its constitution. In its

Aspidistra elatior

heyday in England, where it was as vital to a Victorian sitting room as plush wallpaper. It was called the beer plant. It throve in pubs where it downed many a pint of warm, flat beer (a liquid that many plants seem to like). More politely, however, the aspidistra was known as the parlor palm. It has long, dark leaves that curve, palmlike, from a central cluster.

The incredible tolerance of *Aspidistra elatior* does not hold true for the variety with striped leaves, *variegata*. Like all variegated plants, it needs more sunlight than the plain one does. You may find *elatior* listed as *lurida*. There's nothing lurid about it.

FOLIAGE; EASY; OFFICE

ASPLENIUM NIDUS (Bird's-nest fern, Spleenwort)

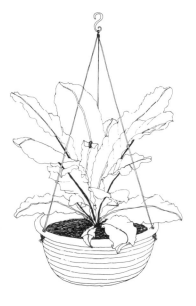

LIGHT — east or west; not south; try north if you need to.

TEMPERATURE — warm, but may take coolish.

HUMIDITY — lots. Try to spray the plant more than once a day.

WATERING — keep the soil moist, but not soggy.

FEEDING — once a month.

SOIL — add sharp sand to the soil so that it doesn't clump around the roots. Be sure the pot has good drainage. *Asplenium* will also grow in soilless material such as bark.

PROPAGATION — since it is difficult to divide the root clump without damaging the plant, it is safest just to enjoy the one you have. If you feel brave, however, you might try rooting the tip of a frond.

Asplenium nidus

Bird's-nest fern doesn't look like most ferns; its fronds are not divided into many leaflets as most ferns' are. Instead, large (maybe two feet long or more), solid, sometimes wavy-edged leaves curve out from a central point. New leaves open deep inside the leaf cluster. Before they uncurl they look like little round eggs in a nest of leaves, hence the common name. The leaves continue to grow as long as the plant is healthy. Do not let water sit in the middle of the cluster or future growth will be lost as the plant rots.

The botanical name *Asplenium* has a common derivation with the word "spleen." The plant was used long ago in treating spleen and liver diseases, except with women patients. It was thought to cause sterility in women.

FOLIAGE; TERRARIUM

BEGONIA

LIGHT — east, west, or shaded south. Lack of good light is a prime reason for failure.

TEMPERATURE — coolish.

HUMIDITY — fairly high; place on pebble tray; spray around (not on) on sunny days; never spray when flowering.

WATERING — keep the soil damp unless otherwise specified below.

FEEDING — every two or three weeks when active; every six weeks when resting, generally in winter.

SOIL — add sand to standard potting soil so it doesn't become too compacted around the roots. Be sure the pot, which can be fairly small, drains well.

PROPAGATION — root stem cuttings in sand or vermiculite. For rhizomatous types, cut off growing tip of rhizome. Cut tip into several chunks and pot the pieces standing up or lying down (the pieces of rhizome, not you). Don't let the soil become soggy — the pieces can rot.

I first came to know begonias when I won little plants year after year for regular attendance at

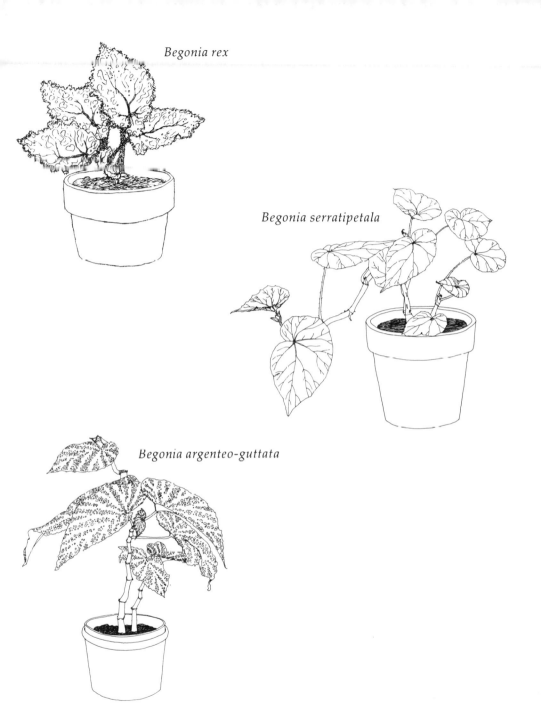

Begonia rex

Begonia serratipetala

Begonia argenteo-guttata

Sunday School. And, I must admit, it took adult apartment living to make me appreciate them.

The begonia family comes in incredible variety. Some are grown for their fascinating leaves, others for beautiful, abundant flowers. They even come with a variety of root structures. With their variety in appearance, however, comes variety in requirements.

The easiest and most reliable begonias are the rhizomatous (be not alarmed — it just means they have an underground stem that behaves like a root in storing food and water). Plant structures, including regular stems, grow from the rhizomes. The root systems, therefore, tend to be small, allowing these begonias to be kept in shallow pots. The beefsteak begonia (*B. feasti*) is rhizomatous. It has large, smooth leaves that are red on the back. The iron cross begonia (*B. masoniana*) is another popular variety; its large leaves are marked with a brownish rough cross.

Because rhizomes are food-storage structures, these begonias can be neglected somewhat and the soil can be left until almost dry before rewatering. When repotting rhizomatous begonias, don't cover the rhizome; leave it above the soil. In some varieties, the rhizome will creep over the side of the pot and send stems out in all directions, giving you a plant that requires living in a hanging basket.

If leaves start to drop, your rhizomatous begonia is probably going into a short rest period. Keep it warm and in dim light, and it should come back stronger than ever.

There are several varieties of miniature or dwarf rhizomatous begonias that will add color to terrariums. Be sure you can get at them to remove the dead flower heads.

Rex begonias (*B. rex*) are grown for their attractive foliage of sharply pointed, colored leaves. Most varieties are reddish with white splotches paralleling the edge of the leaf. Many rex begonias have rhizomatous stems. The rexes require a higher humidity than other begonias: keep them on pebble trays but never spray. They may lose some leaves in winter, but they quickly replace them.

The wax begonias (*B. semperflorens*) are the most colorful and reliable of the flowering begonias. They have roundish, glossy leaves and almost year-round blooms (*semperflorens* means "ever-blooming") in red, pink, or white. The roots are fibrous. They should be kept pot-bound for good flowering, and the soil may be allowed to almost dry. When flowering slows down, prune back branches for new growth, which appears very quickly. Keep growing tips pinched back for bushy growth. You probably will not get more than two or three years from a wax begonia, but cuttings root quickly for fresh plants.

The angel wing begonias, grown primarily for their large, lopsided, pointed leaves, are also fibrous rooted. They produce lovely clusters of salmon, coral, or red flowers, often continuously. One of the most popular, *B. corallina*, has red-backed, spotted leaves; it grows vigorously and needs severe pruning. Some angel wings are good hanging varieties.

The tuberous begonias have magnificent flowers, but I can't recommend them for apartment life because the tubers (another form of specialized stem) must be dried and stored in winter for new spring growth. If you receive one of these begonias as a gift, however, give it more water than you do most varieties, keeping the soil moist.

Begonias do beautifully under artificial light, about fifteen hours of it each day. Be sure that a nighttime temperature drop of five to ten degrees is achieved for good blooms. Avoid crowding the plants.

If, after all this, you are confused about begonias, you're not alone. The thousands of varieties, as well as the new ones appearing all the time, tend to be overwhelming. I suggest you select one you like, making sure you know what kind it is. Try

Billbergia nutans

it out, and if it does well, cheer, and go on from there. Branch out into new types or stick to the ones with which you know you can succeed. The color and charm of begonias will add immeasurably to your apartment plant family.

FOLIAGE; FLOWERING; TERRARIUM; HANGING

BILLBERGIA NUTANS (Living vase plant)

LIGHT — south, east, or west.

TEMPERATURE — warm or coolish.

HUMIDITY — lots; spray regularly.

WATERING — keep the soil moist and the "vase" of leaf cluster filled with water that has sat for a day.

FEEDING — once a month.

SOIL — add sand and chopped peat moss to standard potting soil, or use a soilless mixture.

PROPAGATION — separate and plant the offsets after they have turned somewhat tough and woody.

In general, *Billbergia* gets about the same treatment as *Aechmea*. *Billbergia nutans*, however, is rather smaller than most aechmeas with leaves usually only six or eight inches long. The flower spike, which droops gracefully, is almost psychedelic. It bears blossoms of dark blue and green petals crowned by bright gold anthers, which appear from within red bracts. The flower usually appears in later winter, and the best flowers come when the plant is pot-bound. The flowers last only a week or so. When potting a billbergia, be sure the base of the leaf cluster is above the level of the soil.

FOLIAGE; FLOWERING; EASY

CACTUS

LIGHT — south. Here is your chance to use those south-facing windows in summer without protective curtains unless you detect signs of the plants yellowing from too much light.

TEMPERATURE — warm.

HUMIDITY — normal but spray occasionally in summer.

WATERING — let soil dry completely (this may happen more quickly than you expect) before rewatering thoroughly. Reduce amount used in rewatering during the rest period. Water immediately if you detect any sign of shriveling.

FEEDING — a couple of times, about a month apart, after the resting period is over.

SOIL — add small pebbles and a great deal of sand to standard potting soil, or buy special cactus soil. Use a superabundance of broken pot or pebbles under the soil for very quick drainage. Be sure the soil is packed firmly around the plant.

PROPAGATION — those cacti that branch can have a branch cut off cleanly and potted fairly deeply, with the cut end about two inches down.

Opuntia schickendantzi

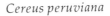

Cereus peruviana

Cacti represent the epitome of succulence, or water-storage ability. Normal leaves and other extraneous structures have been dispensed with, leaving only a functional shape (often delightful) dedicated to holding water, and occasional flowers to guarantee perpetuation of the species. About 1,700 species of cactus are in the family, which originated primarily in dry areas of the New World.

Every shop that carries cacti has its own favorites for sale, from *Lithops* (living stones that look like the decorative pebbles strewn in a dish garden) to *Cephalocereus* (the old man cactus in which the whole thick stem disappears behind a pettable, long, curly, white beard). Just study them all and pick out the one — or ones, if you lean that way — that appeal to you. The desert cacti all get the same general care.

Many apartment cacti will bloom in the environ-

Opuntia species

Opuntia subulata monstrosa

ment you can provide. For some, in fact, the flowers are their only charm (that's personal opinion). The blossoms usually give off a tantalizing but evanescent scent. Desert cacti must be appallingly potbound to bloom. Water more frequently when the plants are flowering.

Cacti in a dry, but open, terrarium cancel out the normal rules, except for good drainage, governing terrariums that are meant to develop humidity. They generally last longer than other terrarium plants unless you overwater. And they grow very slowly so you need not worry about house room. Use a mixture of about two-thirds sand to one-third standard potting soil for the soil layer above the drainage. Water only when the sand-soil is completely dry, but then water thoroughly so that moisture reaches the roots. In winter, when the cacti must rest, place the whole terrarium in a cool, dim place, and water even more sparingly.

You can't bathe cacti as you do other plants, and they don't achieve the miracle of avoiding settling dust, so you still need to keep them clean. Invest in a small, soft paint brush and dust your cacti with it regularly.

There are some nondesert cacti, so be sure you know which kind you select when choosing one. The nondesert cacti, such as orchid cactus (*Epiphyllum*) and *Rhipsalis* are from rain-forest areas and thus require different treatment from desert cacti. Some have branches that dangle, requiring life in a hanging basket. They grow best in orchid-type soil which should never be allowed to dry out completely at the roots, and they enjoy being sprayed often. The traditional Christmas cactus belongs to the rain-forest group. However, I don't recommend it for easygoing apartment life because it generally requires imprisonment in a totally dark closet for carefully timed periods to force it to bloom.

FOLIAGE; FLOWERING; TERRARIUM

CEROPEGIA WOODII (Rosary vine, String of hearts, or Hearts entangled)

LIGHT — east or west or shaded south. If all you have is a north window and you find the plant charming, as I do, go ahead and try it purely as a foliage plant.

TEMPERATURE — coolish, but needs warmth and bright light to bloom.

HUMIDITY — normal.

WATERING — let the soil get dry before rewatering.

> Note: every once in a while, this plant may decide to rest and the fleshy leaves appear to wilt. Give it less water until new stems appear; then return to normal watering.

FEEDING — once a month; more when blooming.

SOIL — mix sand in standard potting soil (about one to four). Be sure the pot has good drainage.

PROPAGATION — root cuttings from stem end. Or you may have small tubers growing by the leaves; cut off several carefully and pot them.

Ceropegia woodii

Hearts entangled (the name I prefer, though you're more apt to find it as rosary vine) is a succulent from Rhodesia. Its Latin name, *Ceropegia*, means "wax fountain," which is beautifully descriptive of the plant. It drapes gracefully over a pot, sometimes hanging down two or more feet. If not allowed to hang freely (as in a terrarium, where the plant does well, but be sure it's reachable for trimming), the stems trail along the ground. The small, heart-shaped leaves are marked with white on top and are soft pink-gray on the back, making hearts entangled an unusual foliage plant. However, if conditions are right (warm and fairly bright), you should get small, pinky-purple, tubelike flowers growing along the stems in summer.

FOLIAGE; FLOWERING; TERRARIUM; HANGING

Chlorophytum elatum

CHLOROPHYTUM ELATUM (Spider plant)

LIGHT — east, west, or shielded south. Try north if that's all you have.

TEMPERATURE — warm.

HUMIDITY — normal apartment air is acceptable but spray the plant often.

WATERING — keep the soil damp. Every two weeks or so let the soil dry before rewatering thoroughly.

FEEDING — once a month.

SOIL — standard potting soil.

PROPAGATION — pot the little plantlets that grow on the ends of long stalks; or divide the root clump and pot pieces separately.

*Chlorophytum elatum,
rooted runner*

The spider plant is an impressive basket plant. Its long, green or green-and-white-striped leaves droop gracefully. Long runners shoot out and bear at their ends miniature spider plants called plantlets. The plant is also called walking anthericum and the airplane plant — extremes in transportation in one plant. It does seem to walk through its natural surroundings — the plantlets take root where they lie, grow into new adults, and send out new runners with unimportant white flowers that develop into new plantlets — all this activity from a plant whose botanical name, *Chlorophytum*, has the undistinguished meaning of "green plant." The plant seems to require being slightly pot-bound in order to have the urge to send out runners.

It's tempting to put the tiny plantlets into a moderate-humidity terrarium, but don't bother. They grow and spread too quickly to justify the trouble of planting and then having to uproot them. A dwarf species, *C. bicheti*, is more suitable for terrariums.

FOLIAGE; EASY; HANGING

CISSUS ANTARCTICA (Kangaroo vine)

CISSUS RHOMBIFOLIA (Grape ivy)

LIGHT — any except direct south.

TEMPERATURE — any.

HUMIDITY — normal, but spray daily.

WATERING — keep the soil moist, although an occasional drying of the soil is beneficial, especially for kangaroo vine.

FEEDING — once a month.

SOIL — standard potting soil.

PROPAGATION — root stem cuttings.

These "ivies" (which aren't in the common ivy family, though *Cissus* means "ivy" in Greek) are among the most useful foliage plants. They are compliant, versatile in where they will grow, and easy to care for.

The kangaroo vine *(Cissus antarctica)* has pointed leaves about three or four inches long. These are light colored when young and dark and leathery when older, with toothed edges and indented veins. The plant comes from kangaroo country, New South Wales in Australia.

Cissus rhombifolia

Cissus rhombifolia has rhombus-shaped (kite-shaped) leaves that grow in threes. New leaves are slightly hairy and have a reddish tinge. This plant comes from the Caribbean area. The name grape ivy is from the clusters of tiny red berries you may be lucky enough to get. There will be too few of them to be useful, but eat them and enjoy their sweet taste.

Both these plants will hang gracefully or climb with ease by tiny tendrils. Help them by using stakes or string. And keep them under firm control with regular trimming.

One warning about grape ivy: the leaves may suddenly start to dry out and fall. This heart-rending slow death can be stopped by transplanting them into a smaller pot. For some reason, grape ivy just doesn't like lots of *lebensraum*.

FOLIAGE; EASY; HANGING OR CLIMBING

CITRUS AURANTIFOLIA (Key lime)

Citrus mitis

CITRUS LIMONIA PONDEROSA (American wonder, or ponderosa, lemon)

CITRUS TAITENSIS (Otaheite orange)

LIGHT — south; shield it in summer. Will look attractive in east or west light but probably will not flower and fruit properly.

TEMPERATURE — must have cool, even cold, nights in winter; warmth in summer. Be sure the room air circulates well.

HUMIDITY — somewhat higher than normal apartment humidity; spray daily except when blossoming.

WATERING — keep the soil moist.

FEEDING — use a mild acidic fertilizer with every second or third watering from the first sign of flower buds until the fruit is developed.

SOIL — standard potting soil.

PROPAGATION — root stem cuttings.

Yes, you can plant the seeds from fruit you eat, but you'll end up with just foliage plants. They won't flower or fruit for years and years. Seedlings will grow best with a bit of help (several hours a day) from a light bulb about fifteen to eighteen inches from the plant.

People have discovered that these fruit trees with their glossy leaves are very attractive indoors. And visitors' gasps of amazement at heavy, full-sized fruit growing on small trees can be truly soul-satisfying.

The citruses are trees, of course, and need control. Size can be limited by keeping them pot-bound. Plan, too, to prune the trees regularly with a sharp knife. Do not crowd the plants.

The trees probably won't produce fruit unless you act as a bee. When the flowers are wide open, pick up the pollen of one blossom with a very soft, small paint brush and touch the brush to another blossom. Go on around the tree, touching the pollen of all blossoms. Some of your artificial cross-pollination efforts should bear fruit.

The fruit of the lime is edible. The American wonder lemon and the orange are more attractive than tasty. You will probably need to put crutches in the pot to support the fruit-bearing branches; although the tree is miniature, the fruit is not.

If the leaves of your citrus turn yellow, it probably needs iron. Feed it a mild solution of the iron product recommended by your favorite plant store.

FOLIAGE; FLOWERING

CLIVIA MINIATA   (Kaffir lily)

LIGHT — any except extremes.

TEMPERATURE — coolish.

HUMIDITY — any.

Clivia miniata

WATERING — in general, let the soil get dry before rewatering; when the plant is blossoming, however, keep the soil moist.

Note: never let water, especially if it contains fertilizer, sit in the heart of the leaves. It will rot the heart, destroying the bloom source.

FEEDING — every week from when new growth starts (about New Year's), until the plant finishes blooming. It eats a great deal during that time.

SOIL — mix sand and extra peat with standard potting soil or use African violet soil. Be sure that the pot drains well. It should be a couple of sizes larger than seems appropriate.

PROPAGATION — it is not only desirable to propagate *Clivia* by separating the offsets (the baby plants attached to the mother at the side) but necessary for the health of the mother plant. Don't do it, however, until the offsets are large and mature. They may be a few years old before they detach themselves far enough for you to cut through the roots. Plant the offsets in pots almost as large as the one the mother plant is in.

The Kaffir lily is one of the few bulb plants I recommend as an apartment plant. It doesn't lose its leaves after blooming even though it is in the same family as *Amaryllis*, which does. Its long, dark, straplike leaves maintain their fan formation through the fall and winter rest period. During that period, let the plant get cold at night and cut down on watering it.

In late winter, stalks appear in the center of the leaf cluster, soon towering over it. Start watering and feeding more, and move the plant to a warmer, slightly brighter location. The stalks then bear magnificent clusters of small, orange or red, amaryllis-shaped flowers. The plant must be fully mature before it blooms (as often happens with nice people), so have patience with the young plants you buy or the offsets you separate. Enjoy the foliage in the meantime.

The roots that develop in an extralarge pot are strong and voracious. The best blooms won't appear until the roots are somewhat pot-bound, so don't dash off to the pot store when you see roots coming through the drainage hole. Eventually you'll separate the offsets and return the original plant to its familiar pot with fresh soil.

FOLIAGE; FLOWERING; EASY

CODIAEUM VARIEGATUM   (Croton)

LIGHT — south, shielded at midday in summer only.

TEMPERATURE — warm.

HUMIDITY — lots; spray daily and keep pot on a pebble tray.

WATERING — keep the soil moist. NEVER let it dry.

FEEDING — once a month.

SOIL — standard potting soil.

PROPAGATION — root leaf cuttings, preferably in sand mixed with soil.

Codiaeum aucubaevolium

The splashed-paint-pot coloring of croton makes it a popular plant. But there are two places it should not be used: if you have children or pets who nibble (the leaves are very poisonous!) or if the only room you have available is already colorful (the leaves are downright garish and will clash with anything but a plain background).

Croton is a shrub in the South where it comes in amazing variety. In looking for apartment crotons, you're apt to find flat leaves, wavy leaves, veined markings, polka dots, red, yellow, pink, orange, or even green — and they are all *Codiaeum variegatum*. Small, dull flowers may grow, but they get lost among the color and might as well be pinched off.

Crotons don't like drafts, but they do want fresh, circulating air. If you use crotons in a terrarium, leave the top off. They grow fairly fast, though, so you won't be able to keep them fenced in for long.

FOLIAGE; TERRARIUM

COLEUS BLUMEI   (Painted, or flame, nettle; Jacob's coat)

LIGHT — east, west, or south (shielded in summer). The color is best in bright light.

TEMPERATURE — warm.

HUMIDITY — lots and constant. Leaves are velvety, so don't spray.

WATERING — keep the soil moist.

FEEDING — once a month.

SOIL — standard potting soil.

PROPAGATION — root tip cuttings, preferably each year for a regular supply of fresh plants.

Coleus blumei

Coleus is another brightly colored plant that requires quiet background colors to look its best. The reds and greens and whites of the leaves are most vivid in sun, but take care, too much sun dulls the leaves. The edges of the leaves are toothed and may be bordered with white, highlighting the other colors.

Plants in sunny positions, of course, need lots of water. *Coleus* will signal that it isn't getting enough by drooping leaves. The humidity in a terrarium is good for it, but be sure there is a deep drainage layer under the soil. Both in terrariums and in pots, *Coleus* needs frequent pruning to keep its exuberant growth under control. It is prone to mealybugs. Rather than trying to combat them, select a couple of clean cuttings and throw away the old plant.

A feathery plume of flowers occasionally rises above the leaves, adding to the attractiveness of *Coleus*, but it is grown primarily for its gay leaves.

FOLIAGE; FLOWERING; EASY; TERRARIUM; WATER

COLUMNEA MICROPHYLLA (Goldfish flower, Costa Rican plant)

LIGHT — east or west or shaded south; if you have a choice, place in the brighter location.

TEMPERATURE — warm.

HUMIDITY — lots; spray the plant daily unless you choose a hairy-leaved variety.

WATERING — keep the soil moist.

FEEDING — every two weeks.

SOIL — add sand to standard potting soil; put a pebble layer in the bottom of the pot for good drainage.

PROPAGATION — plant stem cuttings; cover pot with plastic bag to insure high humidity. Leaf cuttings will root but they grow extremely slowly.

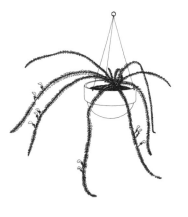

Columnea microphylla

Like its relative the African violet, *Columnea* is a plant that seems to grow well for a specific person or not, just as the plant chooses. If you're successful, however, you'll have a magnificent addition to your collection.

Columnea comes in both upright and hanging varieties. If you don't know which yours is when you buy it, you'll soon find out. The long stems bear tiny, gray-green leaves in pairs opposite each other. Trim back a young plant to make it produce more stems and grow thick.

At random intervals through spring, summer, and even fall, vivid, orangy red, tubelike flowers appear along the stem. Columnea's flowers look like goldfish.

In its natural jungle habitat, *Columnea* acts like an epiphyte (air plant) and grows from mossy branches or anywhere that rotting vegetation lies. That situation gives the plant just what it needs: lots of water with no chance of the roots getting soggy.

FOLIAGE; FLOWERING; TERRARIUM; HANGING

CORDYLINE TERMINALIS (Ti plant)

LIGHT — east or west.

TEMPERATURE — warm.

HUMIDITY — spray regularly.

WATERING — keep the soil moist.

FEEDING — once a month.

SOIL — standard potting soil.

PROPAGATION — plant inch-long sections of stem horizontally. Keep them warm and damp, and be patient.

You may find this attractive foliage plant as *Dracaena terminalis*. The difference between *Cordyline* and *Dracaena* is significant only to plants and botanists. Their care and feeding are similar.

The ti plant is Hawaiian. The most frequently sold variety has red leaves, but it also comes in green, with red edges, and with cream markings. Most turn plain green when they get old. The leaves are long and arch nicely. They are more rounded in shape than the leaves of most dracaenas. They grow in palm fashion, spiraling up a single stem. Also palmlike is the not-so-desirable habit of the lower leaves dying. However, most of the varieties available in shops these days have been bred for tenacious lower leaves. If they do drop, and the plant begins to look top heavy, cut off the top and air-layer it to gain a new plant.

FOLIAGE; WATER

Cordyline terminalis

CRASSULA ARGENTEA (Jade plant)

LIGHT — east or west; will often accept north, but generally needs several hours of sun each day.

TEMPERATURE — coolish.

HUMIDITY — normal.

WATERING — let the soil be dry for two or three days before rewatering thoroughly.

FEEDING — a couple of times when fresh growth starts, preferably with a low nitrogen content fertilizer.

SOIL — add sand and pebbles to standard potting soil.

PROPAGATION — root leaf or stem cuttings.

The jade plant is one of the frequently grown succulent plants. Its thick stem and fleshy leaves are a nice addition to a dry dish garden or terrarium. Seen in such containers, it's hard to believe that in its native South Africa the jade plant is a hardy shrub. There's nothing about the indoors, though, to keep you from growing a shrub there, if you have years to wait and a half-time sunny place to keep it.

The major danger to the jade plant is your own tendency to overwater. That will rot most succulents because they just can't handle their internally stored water plus extra outside water.

Crassula arborescens has also been called jade plant. It looks like a fat, miniature tree, which in strong light turns reddish-brown along the leaf edges.

FOLIAGE; TERRARIUM

Crassula argentea

CROSSANDRA INFUNDIBULIFORMIS
(Firecracker flower)

LIGHT — east or west; good winter sun is a must for flowering; protect from direct spring and summer sun.

TEMPERATURE — warm.

HUMIDITY — lots; spray daily and keep on a pebble tray. High humidity is vital for healthy plants.

WATERING — keep the soil moist.

FEEDING — two or three times a year.

SOIL — mix peat moss with standard potting soil; be sure the pot drains well.

Crossandra infundibuliformis

PROPAGATION — root stem cuttings.

You'll note from the "must" and "vital" above that *Crossandra* is hardly in the easy category. But if you can maintain warmth, high humidity, and good but not direct sun, you'll have a plant to brag about.

The firecracker flower is as vivid as its name. Balls of bright orangy-salmon flowers — often several heads at once — burst forth in spring and summer. *Crossandra* must be an incredible sight in its native India where it grows as a shrub.

When not in bloom, a healthy plant is still beautiful because the wide, pointed leaves are dark green and glossy, similar to gardenia leaves. It may lose some leaves in winter but will soon regain them.

Because of its need for high humidity, *Crossandra* quite likes life in a terrarium. However, be sure to use only a wide-mouthed container. You must be able to reach the plant to remove dead flower heads.

FLOWERING; FOLIAGE; TERRARIUM

CYPERUS ALTERNIFOLIUS (Umbrella plant)

LIGHT — any except extremes.

TEMPERATURE — cool.

HUMIDITY — lots; spray often. If you keep it on a pebble tray (and you should), sink the pot into the pebbles instead of resting it on top.

WATERING — keep the soil WET, and stand the pot in a saucer of water if not using a pebble tray.

FEEDING — every two or three weeks, except in winter.

SOIL — standard potting soil.

PROPAGATION — divide the root clump or cut off a leaf group and root in water.

This is the only really and truly water-growing

Cyperus alternifolius

plant in this book. It likes all the water it can get — on leaves, roots, stems, anywhere. It's a sister plant to the papyrus of the Nile River. Papyrus (*C. papyrus*) is sometimes grown indoors but it reaches for the sky in a way that would overwhelm most apartments.

If *Cyperus* doesn't get enough water, the leaf tips easily turn brown. Trim off the tips with scissors if that happens.

This plant has long, grasslike leaves that grow in groups from a central stem, like the ribs in an umbrella. It generally reaches two or three feet high. Dwarf varieties are available, such as a dramatic one with linear white stripes on the green leaves.

The plant may develop little whitish-brown flowers on longish stems which rise from the center of the umbrella-rib leaves. They look a bit like sparkler fire.

FOLIAGE; EASY; WATER

Davallia

DAVALLIA (Rabbit-foot, or deer-foot, fern, Ball fern)

LIGHT — east or west; will accept north.

TEMPERATURE — warm.

HUMIDITY — lots, like all ferns.

WATERING — keep the soil moist.

FEEDING — once a month.

SOIL — add sand to standard potting soil; be sure the pot drains well.

PROPAGATION — divide the root clump or break off and pot one of the furry feet.

I'm not sure that good luck extends by analogy from rabbits' feet to rabbit-foot ferns, but it's worth a try. Davallias are charming ferns that make people ask if they can have a piece of the rabbit — an easy way to keep the plant a reasonable size (it's easier than giving away kittens).

The rabbit feet of *Davallia* are long, furry rhizomes, specialized stems from which fronds grow, seemingly at random. The feet grow from the base and droop lazily over the side of the pot so that the carrotlike fronds may stick out in almost any direction.

Davallias are sometimes called ball ferns because in the past they were often sold as balls of furry rhizome which began to grow when watered. These ferns tend to be smaller than the other ferns, rarely reaching more than ten inches high. *Davallia mariesii* is even smaller than most and does very well in high-humidity terrariums.

FOLIAGE; TERRARIUM; HANGING

DIEFFENBACHIA (Dumb cane)

LIGHT — any but south in summer; likes some sun occasionally.

TEMPERATURE — warm.

HUMIDITY — fairly high; spray daily and keep on a pebble tray.

WATERING — let soil dry between thorough waterings. Overwatering may rot the plant.

FEEDING — once a month.

SOIL — standard potting soil.

PROPAGATION — root leaf cuttings or root sections of lower stem after air-layering the top.

Dieffenbachia maculata

Dieffenbachia isn't called dumb cane because it's a dumb plant (although I personally am not so sure) but because the leaves are toxic, rendering the one who chews them speechless for a couple of days. The tongue and throat swell and are painful. Fortunately, the leaves are large, dramatic, and few, so there's little temptation to absentmindedly remove one and chew it.

This can be a fairly large feature plant in your apartment. It can reach five feet tall but is more likely to be two or three feet. The large leaves are dark green, spotted or lightly striped with white, cream, or light green. They grow from one central cane from which bottom leaves occasionally die, so that eventually you are left with a top-heavy plant. At that time, you can try rooting the whole healthy top.

It may lose some of its leaves when resting in winter. Don't panic; they will quickly grow again when through resting.

FOLIAGE; EASY; OFFICE; WATER

DIZYGOTHECA ELEGANTISSIMA (False, or finger, aralia; Threadleaf)

LIGHT — east or west; be sure it has a fair amount of light when the leaves are actively growing.

TEMPERATURE — warm to coolish.

HUMIDITY — lots; keep it on a pebble tray, and spray often.

WATERING — keep the soil moist except every third or fourth watering, when you should let the soil dry before rewatering.

FEEDING — every two weeks when actively growing.

SOIL — add a little chopped peat to standard potting soil.

PROPAGATION — plant stem cuttings.

Dizygotheca elegantissima

I'd like to call *Dizygotheca* "dark lace." It's a much more fitting name than the bland false, or finger, aralia. "Finger" is appropriate, however, because the seven to ten very narrow leaflets that make up the compound leaf are like the fingers of a slender, rather skeletal hand. The leaflets are a dark greenish-purple that is almost black.

Dizygotheca is a tropical plant from the New Hebrides. It needs a good deal of moisture and light. A lack of either will cause a dropping of the lower leaves, especially unfortunate because they never grow again, leaving you with an embarrassingly bare woody stem. You can, however, cut off the top of the plant, root it, and give it lots of tender, loving care until it takes hold.

False aralia (it used to be considered a member of genus *Aralia*, which has large, ivylike leaves) is fairly slow growing, making it useful as a tallish plant in a terrarium, but it can reach three or four feet tall and look like a lacy tree.

FOLIAGE; TERRARIUM

DRACAENA FRAGRANS   (Corn plant)

DRACAENA GODSEFFIANA   (Gold-dust plant or Florida Beauty)

DRACAENA MARGINATA   (Red-edged dracaena)

DRACAENA WARNECKII

LIGHT — any except extremes.

TEMPERATURE — prefers warm but can stand cold.

HUMIDITY — normal but spray daily.

WATERING — keep the soil moist. Let it dry somewhat when the plant is resting.

FEEDING — once a month.

SOIL — standard potting soil. Be sure the pot drains well.

PROPAGATION — very difficult! Dracaenas are reluctant to grow new roots and generally rot before giving in. They can't be divided (except *D. godseffiana*) because they are single-stemmed plants. Some people cut the tops off of old, bedraggled plants and root them, but the product is a misshapen creature. If you try that, also try cutting the leafless stem into sections and planting them. Good luck. I suggest you air-layer the top or buy new plants.

The dracaenas are often called dragon plants. The

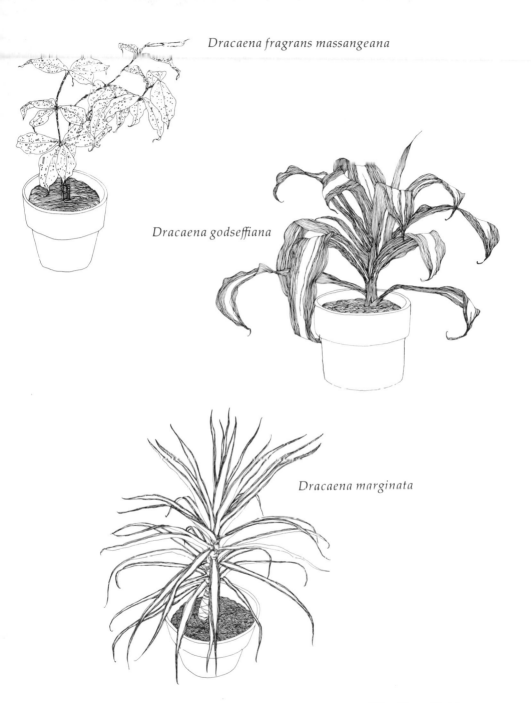

Dracaena fragrans massangeana

Dracaena godseffiana

Dracaena marginata

biggest one, the dragon tree of the Canary Islands, weeps dragon's blood, a dark red resin used as a varnish for fine violins. The plants belong, oddly enough, to the lily family.

The first time I saw *Dracaena fragrans*, I thought the greenhouse keeper had planted corn on a work bench. The plant was higher than an elephant's eye and looked as if it would yield golden cobs any minute. *Dracaena fragrans* itself is solid green. A very popular variety is *D. fragrans massangeana*, with wide whitish bands down the leaves. These plants require less light than the other dracaenas and grow well in offices. *Massangeana*, however, maintains its stripe better with stronger light.

The corn plant, in common with the other dracaenas, tends to lose its lower leaves as it gets older, and the leaves are not replaced. So, after some years, you are left with a top-heavy leaf structure balanced on a thin stalk. Top-heaviness can be effective, however, with *D. marginata*. I've seen one bare-bottomed, red-edged dracaena that looked like an exotic bird perched on a branch ready for flight. *Dracaena marginata* is sometimes called *Cordyline marginata*. *Cordyline* is a very close relative and a distinction between them is often not made.

The gold-dust plant has rounder leaves than the other dracaenas. The leaves are sprinkled with gold or cream. It starts small and grows very slowly, a trait making it useful in terrariums. Wipe the leaves with a damp sponge frequently to stop bugs. *Dracaena godseffiana*, unlike the others, has several slender stems and can have its root clump divided for propagation.

Dracaena warneckii, also called *D. deremensis warnecki*, has long, striped leaves like the corn plant variety. But the leaves aren't as broad; they're more sword-shaped. In color, they are dark, almost bluish-green with a narrow strip.

In reading what other writers had to say about dracaenas, I found an amazing variety of instructions. Quite different care seems to work well for different people, indicating that these useful plants are very tolerant of human frailties. Be kind and they'll accept almost anything you offer. Be sure to keep the leaves clean.

FOLIAGE; EASY; TERRARIUM; OFFICE; WATER

EPISCIA (Flame Violet)

Episcia cupreata

LIGHT — east, west, or away from a south window.

TEMPERATURE — warm. They don't like a temperature drop at night.

HUMIDITY — lots, even more than African violets. Don't spray, because the leaves are hairy; keep on pebble trays.

WATERING — keep the soil moist.

FEEDING — every two weeks when actively growing.

SOIL — standard potting soil; be sure the pot has good drainage.

PROPAGATION — root runners or stem cuttings. You can anchor the curve of the stem (near a leaf) into the soil with a hair pin or half a paper clip (be careful not to crush the stem). Roots will form at the curve and stem.

The leaf of the episcia may have been a model for the brightly colored plush wallpaper of Victorian times. These plants are also called flame violets, but, although they are in the same family, the red flowers bear little resemblance to African violets.

The velvety-haired episcia leaf is dark with distinct veins. In many varieties, an almost fluorescent vein structure leaps out in contrast to the dark background. These plants are generally grown for their delicately beautiful foliage. Episcias stay in full leaf year round if they are kept warm. If the leaves do fall off in winter, however, cut down on watering and keep the humidity and temperature high until new growth appears. Pinching runners will also lead to more of the bright red, orange, white, or purplish flowers if you want the plant for blooms as well as foliage.

Episcias can be upright pot plants, useful even in terrariums. But they make beautiful hanging plants, too. Stems shoot off sideways from trailing runners, creating a striking tangle of color.

More and more hybrids of *Episcia* are appearing on the market these days because they are always pretty, even when not in bloom, and they are easier to grow than African violets.

FOLIAGE; FLOWERING; TERRARIUM; HANGING

EUPHORBIA SPLENDENS   (Crown of thorns)

Euphorbia splendens bojeri

LIGHT — east or west. Needs some sun daily to flower well. It rests in early winter gathering strength for flowering, so put it in shade until buds appear.

TEMPERATURE — coolish.

HUMIDITY — unlike most succulents, crown of thorns doesn't like very dry air. Give it an occasional spray mist.

WATERING — let the soil dry before rewatering. It will let you know if you are overwatering by rather pointedly dropping its leaves. Water a little more during flowering, a little less during its rest period.

FEEDING — once a month.

SOIL — mix sand with potting soil.

PROPAGATION — cut several inches off a branch end and pot fairly deeply.

Legend has it that this *Euphorbia* was used to make the crown of thorns placed on Jesus' head, but since it is originally from Madagascar, that seems unlikely.

This spiny succulent is related to the poinsettia, which I'm not including in this book because it requires specially timed hours of light and dark to bring it to its familiar Christmas splendor. (If you receive one as a gift, just read and follow the instructions that come with it.)

Crown of thorns throws out its red bract "flowers" with just a little attention from you. The flowers appear among the leaves and spines on and off throughout the year except during its short rest period in winter when you should cut back on watering. You can do almost anything to keep the plant (which is basically a shrub) a reasonable size, from pruning it drastically to twisting the branches together to give it a gnarled appearance.

FOLIAGE; FLOWERING; EASY

FATSHEDERA LIZEI   (Tree ivy)

LIGHT — east, west, or north; not south.

TEMPERATURE — cool.

HUMIDITY — any, but, like most plants, it appreciates extra moisture in the air.

WATERING — keep soil moist.

FEEDING — once a month.

SOIL — standard potting soil; must have good drainage.

PROPAGATION — root stem cuttings cut just below where a leaf joins the stem.

Fatshedera lizei

At the beginning of this century, botanists in France developed a sturdy, new house plant. The combination of *Fatsia japonica*, a Japanese aralia, and *Hedera helix*, English ivy, became *Fatshedera lizei*. The hybrid is often called tree ivy or climbing aralia. It twines like the ivy (but without aerial roots) and has leaves that are star-shaped like ivy but are as large as the aralia's.

The plant has a thin stem that seems to go on forever, so it needs support. If you grow it at the back of a planter on a lightweight trellis, it can form a leafy backdrop for other plants.

Fatshedera tends to get scruffy-looking after a winter in semidarkness. Rather than trying to save it, take some cuttings and start new plants. They grow so quickly you won't have time to miss the old one.

A variegated form of *Fatshedera* is available with creamy markings on the leaves. Like all variegated plants, it needs more light than plain green plants do, and it grows more slowly than the standard variety.

FOLIAGE; EASY; OFFICE; WATER; CLIMBING

Ficus lyrata

FICUS BENJAMINA (Weeping, or Indian, fig)

FICUS ELASTICA (India rubber plant)

FICUS LYRATA (Fiddleleaf, or banjo, fig)

FICUS PUMILA (Creeping fig)

LIGHT — any except extremes.

TEMPERATURE — warm.

HUMIDITY — normal but spray daily.

WATERING — keep the soil slightly moist, somewhat dryer in winter. Be very careful not to overwater: the large-leaved species turn brown very easily and irreparably.

FEEDING — once a month.

SOIL — standard potting soil.

PROPAGATION — the India rubber plant and the fiddleleaf fig should be air-layered if they get too leggy, keeping only the top as your main plant. Air-layering will give you extra plants: the bottom part throws out new shoots which can be rooted. Root the stem cuttings of weeping and creeping figs.

The figs are among the most popular and reliable apartment plants. They belong to the same genus as the edible fig and the huge banyan of India,

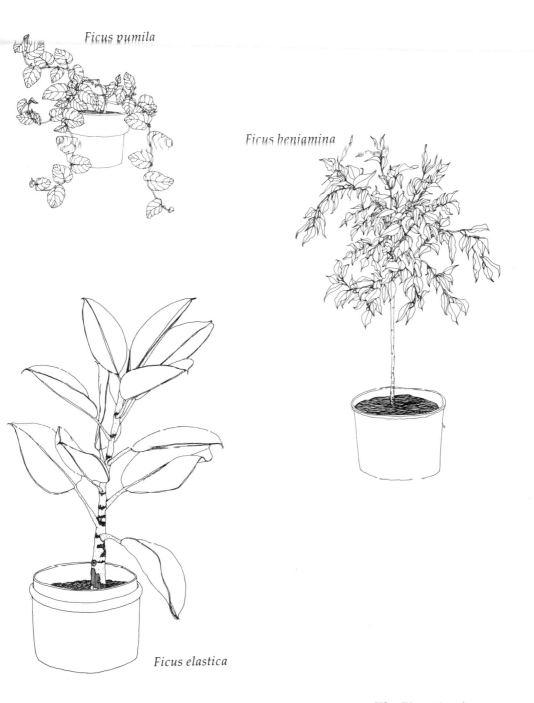

Ficus pumila

Ficus benjamina

Ficus elastica

which produces trunklike aerial roots to such an extent that one tree may be almost half a mile in circumference. Instead of an apartment-dwelling plant, you could have a plant-dwelling apartment. The indoor figs, however, are rather more circumspect in their growing habits.

Ficus benjamina from Southeast Asia has recently become one of the most popular large and dramatic plants bought for apartments; somehow, weeping figs and condominiums go together. The weeping fig is distinctly a tree, with a single trunk. The small, shiny leaves droop in a graceful way. If they fall, which they do occasionally, they replace themselves quickly, so don't get out the pruning shears. The weeping fig grows quickly and may need a supporting stake in the pot if the trunk begins to lean.

The familiar India rubber plant, *F. elastica*, has a rather more stern appearance than the weeping fig. For centuries before Brazil discovered rubber trees, *F. elastica* was man's source of rubber gum. It has a thick, juicy stem up which large, glossy leaves grow in a spiral. The roundish leaves may be a foot long. They should be kept very clean but not shined with leaf oils. If in doubt about watering, keep the soil rather more dry than wet because the leaves turn brown easily and don't repair themselves. Water, wash, and spray only with room-temperature water. Pruning the top of the plant — a heart-rending experience — will encourage the development of multiple stems. This *Ficus* survives in dim light better than the others and will thrive in an office environment if only one person waters it.

The fiddleleaf fig, *F. lyrata* or *pandurata*, is quite like the India rubber plant except the leaves are viol-shaped and soft looking, and they have distinct veins. The leaves may reach eighteen inches long, and should be washed often.

The creeping fig, *F. pumila* or *repens*, is another small-leaved species when young; leaves on an old plant are much larger. The aerial roots by which this fig climbs are very strong and require little encouragement to cling to surfaces. When climbing, the creeping fig holds its leaves flat, parallel to the climbing surface. It likes to spread, so prune firmly to keep it under control.

FOLIAGE; EASY; OFFICE; HANGING OR CLIMBING
(F. pumila)

FITTONIA ARGYRONEURA (Mosaic plant, Nerve plant)

LIGHT — any but extremes; try for east or west or shaded south.

TEMPERATURE — warm; drops leaves if temperature becomes too cold.

HUMIDITY — wants very high humidity; spray daily and keep on pebble tray. If it starts to wilt, revive it by putting a plastic bag over it.

WATERING — keep the soil moist; must not get dry.

FEEDING — once a month.

SOIL — standard potting soil.

PROPAGATION — root a stem cutting several inches

Fittonia argyroneura

long. The stems sometimes root of their own accord; you can then separate the plants.

The pretty, low-growing fittonias look like the creation of a coloring-book artist. They have no gradations of color — just solid green with very distinct veins in white. The veins give rise to the popular name of mosaic plant; it's as though bits of green glass are held together by white glue. The name "nerve plant" may be descriptive, but it makes the plant sound fussy, which it isn't.

The fittonias are from Peru and are named for two Fitton sisters who wrote on botany in Ireland in the 1800s. Useful plants, they can be grown individually or as ground cover to hide the soil in the pot of a large, tall-growing plant. They reside there happily (if the humidity is high enough) in the shade, sometimes draping slightly over the edge of the pot. They may produce bract "flowers," but these are unimportant compared to the foliage. Pinch back the growing tips to keep the plant full and shapely.

Fittonia argyroneura is sometimes considered a variety of *F. verschaffeltii*, which has bright reddish-purple "glue" between the green bits. The green bits are smaller in *argyroneura* than they are in *verschaffeltii*.

FOLIAGE; TERRARIUM

HEDERA HELIX (English ivy)

LIGHT — any except extremes.

TEMPERATURE — cool.

HUMIDITY — fairly high; spray daily.

WATERING — keep the soil moist, but an occasional drying out does no harm.

FEEDING — once a month.

SOIL — standard potting soil.

PROPAGATION — root cuttings several inches long.

English ivy is one of the popular plants indoors or out. It softens barren spots, grows exuberantly with little encouragement, and has become part of our heritage.

Choose your spot for English ivy and it will co-operate — around a window, dangling prettily from a hanging pot, up string for a room divider, or lying on the surface of a large pot. Many varieties are available. Some have small, feathery leaves. One has leaves so deeply indented they look like chicken's feet. Glacier ivy has white edges outlining the usual lobed leaf shape. This variety requires more water and a cooler temperature than the others. The hybrid ivies have been developed specially for indoor life and so are more likely to do well than one you collect from outdoors.

Give your ivy a regular bath in the kitchen sink to keep red spider mites away. If you have the plant trained up a rough wall, where it clings by tiny, sticky roots, you'll need to spray it often with cool water. All ivies need frequent pinching to keep them under control.

FOLIAGE; EASY; WATER; HANGING AND CLIMBING

Hedera helix

Helxine soleirolii

HELXINE SOLEIROLII   (Baby's tears, Irish moss)

LIGHT — north, away from east or west light; likes shade; can even take dark corners for a while; keep it out of full sun.

TEMPERATURE — coolish.

HUMIDITY — lots; spray regularly two or three times a week.

WATERING — keep the soil moist; can tolerate its toes sitting in water.

FEEDING — once a month.

SOIL — standard potting soil.

PROPAGATION — cut a chunk (roots and all) out of existing pot; plant it in a smaller one; let it grow; repeat, *ad infinitum.*

"Ground cover" is an inadequate description of this charming, lacy mat of microscopic, bright green leaves. Planted by itself, baby's tears runs rampant over the pot, with some stems standing "tall" (all of an inch or so) and others draped over the side. In England, the plant is called "mind your own business" because of its habit of creeping unobtrusively into every corner or curve, even where it isn't wanted. It is very effective at soil level in a tall plant's pot or under larger plants in a humid terrarium. Watch it, though, because it tends to strangle its terrarium mates.

Baby's tears thinks it's a tree and may shed its miniature leaves each year, but it soon grows new ones. Like a tree, too, its roots go deep in the soil. When cutting out a chunk to put in another pot, be sure to cut deep enough to get the total root length.

Some garden shops now carry a plant called English baby's tears. It is bigger, with leaves three or four times the size of helxine's.

FOLIAGE; EASY; TERRARIUM

HOWEA   (Kentia palm, Fan palm)

LIGHT — east or west; keep out of full sun.

TEMPERATURE — warm to coolish.

HUMIDITY — lots; spray often.

WATERING — keep the soil moist and rewater thoroughly each time. NEVER let the roots dry or the leaf tips will turn brown.

FEEDING — monthly during spring and summer only.

SOIL — standard potting soil; be sure the pot drains well.

PROPAGATION — must be grown from seeds, so it's silly to bother.

Howea forsteriana

Not many plants of the large palm family are suitable for growing indoors, but the Kentia palms, from Lord Howe Island near New Guinea, do beautifully — if you have room. In their island home, they reach sixty feet, but inside they grow to only five or ten. If you're in an old building with high ceilings, you can let *Howea forsteriana* have its freedom to grow. If they are lowish, you'd better stick to *H. belmoreana* — sometimes called the curly palm. It is shorter and spreads out more.

The howeas were the original potted palms, but don't wrinkle your nose. Their spreading, bright green fronds are lovely if kept under control. Keep the plant in a fairly small pot. Repot once a year or every other year. Take advantage of having it out of its pot (and held by someone else) to trim off some roots, because plants only grow to the extent that they have roots to support growth (a principle of bonzai).

If it has to contend with drafts and dry soil, howea's leaf tips turn brown. Using an artistic eye, clip the ends so that the plants keep their fan shape.

FOLIAGE; OFFICE

HOYA CARNOSA (Wax plant)

Hoya carnosa

LIGHT — bright — east or west; south in winter.

TEMPERATURE — warm.

HUMIDITY — normal; spray often when not in bloom.

WATERING — keep soil moist in spring and summer when the plant is growing and flowering; let it dry out between waterings in winter when the plant is resting; otherwise, it won't bloom properly.

FEEDING — every two weeks except in winter.

SOIL — add sand to standard potting soil. Be sure the pot drains well; roots must not sit in soggy water.

PROPAGATION — root stem cuttings of previous year's new growth in water or soil.

Important: do not remove faded blossoms from HOYA. *The next bunch of sweetly fragrant flowers grows from the old.*

The thick, waxy leaves of the *Hoya* can be green, white, cream, or blushing pink, as well as a combination of these colors. When you buy the plant in a shop, it may look like a low upright plant, but it soon becomes a twining vine, rather unusual for a thick-leaved plant. Left to hang from a basket, the stems can become somewhat bedraggled looking, but that's when the blossoms are best. Fastening the vines upward on a support — making the plant a climber instead of a hanger — keeps it tidier. You can also train the vines around windows as long as they get enough light.

The small, pinkish-white blossoms have red markings and give off a beautiful scent at night. Keep the plant somewhat pot-bound for the best flowers. Never let the roots sit in water; in their native Queensland, Australia, hoyas grow on quickly draining, moss-covered tree branches. If you let the plant get too dry in winter, the thick leaves will alert you by shriveling slightly.

FOLIAGE; FLOWERING; EASY; HANGING AND CLIMBING

IMPATIENS SULTANII   (Patient plant, Busy Lizzie, Patient Lucy)

LIGHT — east, west, or protected south. You may also have luck with a bright north light.

TEMPERATURE — cool.

HUMIDITY — normal but appreciates occasional spraying or resting on a pebble tray.

WATERING — keep the soil moist.

FEEDING — every two or three weeks when actively growing and flowering; these activities happen simultaneously so at this time the plant needs all the energy it can get.

SOIL — standard potting soil.

PROPAGATION — root stem cuttings in water or soil; don't water much when in soil. You can't divide the root clump because, although the plant looks bushy and full, it is basically a single-stemmed plant. You can also plant seeds if *you're* patient.

Impatiens sultanii

Funny things happen to language. This plant was given the name *Impatiens,* meaning, of course, "impatient," because the seed pods explode when ripe. But somehow in common parlance the name reversed itself, lost its "Im-," and became patient plant or patient Lucy. There is, however, nothing patient about it. It grows in a great hurry, giving it another common name — busy Lizzie.

Impatiens comes in amazing variety. The scallop-edged, pointed leaves can be light green, dark green, and variegated. The inch-wide, flat flowers, which appear on and off in winter, can be white, pink, red, purple, orange, and even day-glo, the fluorescent orange color used on military aircraft markings. All of the colors seem to glow under artificial light. You can also find *Impatiens* with double blossoms.

The flowers develop from heart-shaped buds hanging from their own short stems in the middle of a leaf group. The flowers are most abundant if the plant is somewhat pot-bound.

Because the plant grows so freely, you'll want to prune it to keep its shape. Feel free to give away all the pruned cuttings you want; it's easy to have too much *Impatiens* in an apartment. If you decide to let the plant grow, however, you'll need to give some support to the tall stems. They are somewhat succulent and can be brittle when older, especially if the leaves are in full flourish.

FLOWERING; FOLIAGE; EASY

MARANTA LEUCONEURA (Prayer plant)

LIGHT — any except south.

TEMPERATURE — warm.

HUMIDITY — the higher the better; spray the plant daily if possible; keep pot on a pebble tray.

WATERING — keep the soil moist except in winter, when you should reduce watering for six or eight weeks and let the soil dry between waterings.

FEEDING — once a month except in winter.

SOIL — add chopped peat to standard potting soil or use African violet soil.

PROPAGATION — root leaf cuttings or divide roots of a large clump.

Maranta leuconeura

Prayer plants do pray. When the sun goes down, the leaves arch upward, cupped like praying hands. They remain that way until dawn. In nature, the praying lets moisture that has collected on the leaves run down the stem and into the roots.

The large leaves are oval in shape and marked with a symmetrical pattern of purplish splotches that turn brown as the leaves age. Some marantas have red, white, or cream fish-bone markings on the leaves. The plant doesn't like to be crowded, so keep the pot away from others. They do quite well, however, in a terrarium, if there is room for the leaves to move up and down. Prayer plants seem to be a staple in dish gardens bought at florists.

The plants of genus *Calathea* are similar to those of genus *Maranta* and are often mistaken for them. They have the same requirements as marantas. The arrowroot, *M. arundinacea*, is the plant that yields tapioca and is sometimes grown as an indoor plant. The prayer plant has been called false arrowroot.

FOLIAGE; EASY; TERRARIUM

MONSTERA DELICIOSA (Swiss cheese plant; Mexican breadfruit; Split-leaf, or window-leaf, philodendron)

LIGHT — any except bright sun; grows comfortably even in dark corners.

TEMPERATURE — warm.

HUMIDITY — normal; spray the leaves daily.

WATERING — keep the soil moist except for an occasional drying out. Be sure not to let the plant sit in water because its overlarge leaves get charred tips in a proportionately overlarge fashion from overwatering.

FEEDING — once a month.

SOIL — add peat to standard potting soil or use African violet soil.

PROPAGATION — root stem cuttings in water or soil; this is especially effective if aerial roots are attached to the stem giving the rooting a head start. Put all but the leaves inside the pot and fill the spaces with soil.

Have a large living room or office hallway? Try the delicious monster, *Monstera deliciosa*. It's a

Monstera deliciosa

bold plant that, when full-grown, cannot be ignored.

When you ask for this plant in a shop, don't be surprised if you are given a small plant with leaves that look like a plain old philodendron. Monstera's leaves don't develop the deep indentations, which have led the plant to be called window-leaf or split-leaf philodendron, until they are mature. The longer they live, and the larger they grow, the deeper the cuts, as if there were supplied only so much leaf material to be distributed over a larger and larger area. In a natural habitat, the holes keep the leaves from being torn apart by hurricane winds. The leaves, which rise from the pot on thick stems, can reach two or even three feet across.

You can keep the plant from overwhelming your room by trimming the roots when you repot. The aerial roots, however, are useful for climbing on bark supports — another way to keep the plant within bounds.

The leaves, of course, are the striking feature of *Monstera*. Keep them glistening for the best effect. Don't use commercial leaf-shining oils; a mild soap-and-water solution does just as well without clogging the pores if you rinse the leaves afterwards. Between full-fledged baths, dust the leaves occasionally.

It is very unlikely that you'll ever see the large, edible fruit that gives *Monstera* the name bread-fruit.

FOLIAGE; EASY; OFFICE; CLIMBING

NEOMARICA (Apostle plant, Fan iris)

LIGHT — any except extremes; prefers some sun daily.

TEMPERATURE — coolish.

HUMIDITY — lots; spray regularly.

WATERING — keep the soil moist, almost wet.

FEEDING — once a month.

Neomarica northiana

SOIL — standard potting soil. Be sure the pot drains well so it can handle the extra water without making the roots soggy.

PROPAGATION — divide the root clump of mature plants. You may also get small plantlets developing on the flower stem. Pin them down in the soil of a nearby pot with a hair pin. After roots develop, cut the stem from the mother plant.

Tradition says that *Neomarica* is called the apostle plant, or twelve apostles, for one of two reasons. One, there are usually twelve of the swordlike leaves making up the fan of foliage. Two, after the twelve leaves have developed, one turns brown "in betrayal." But it shouldn't; check your care technique if it happens.

When you ask for *Neomarica* (sometimes called *Marica*), you'll be given *N. gracilis* or *N. northiana*. The latter has leaves up to two feet long and produces an orchid-iris-like blossom about four inches across. The former is smaller, in leaves and blossoms. The flowers are so brief in their stay — only about a day — that fan iris barely makes it into the flowering category. But while the flower lasts, it gives off a lovely fragrance. And it's soon followed by another.

FOLIAGE; FLOWERING; EASY

NEPHROLEPIS EXALTATA (Boston, ladder, or sword fern)

LIGHT — east or west; will accept north all year round and south in winter. Like all ferns, does well under artificial light.

TEMPERATURE — coolish.

HUMIDITY — lots; spray daily; keep on deep pebble tray.

WATERING — keep the soil moist.

FEEDING — every two or three weeks.

Nephrolepis exaltata

SOIL — mix sand with standard potting soil. Be sure the pot drains well.

PROPAGATION — divide the root clump when repotting, or plant the wirelike runners that grow from the base (they aren't dead stems even though they seem to be). These runners may root themselves, in which case just lift out the young plant (with its young roots) and give it a pot of its own.

In the 1700s a ship arrived in Boston from the West Indies. On board was a stowaway plant that later became the American equivalent of the hardy, undemanding British *Aspidistra*. Every self-respecting living room possessed (or was possessed by) a Boston fern. Boston, or ladder, or sword, ferns lost their popularity in the first half of this century, but they are coming into their own again.

Horticulturists have developed some wonderful varieties. My favorite is Fluffy Ruffles. Instead of four- or five-inch-wide fronds that need plenty of room to cascade, Fluffy has almost erect and very lacy fronds of compact leaflets. It looks as if you had crimped all the leaflets of the classic Boston fern together in a ruffle. The Whitman variety also has lacy fronds but may revert to the standard Boston-fern type. Cut off those atavistic fronds as soon as they appear or the whole plant will revert.

As with all ferns, clip any frond that turns brown. That and an occasional bath for the whole plant should keep it healthy, for a while. Eventually, unless you are very lucky, so many fronds will have died in the center of the clump that the plant just doesn't look full anymore. Divide the root or plant runners and start over. Trying to rejuvenate the old plant is hopeless.

FOLIAGE; TERRARIUM; HANGING

PANDANUS   (Screwpine)

LIGHT — north, east, or west; but not direct sun.

TEMPERATURE — warm.

HUMIDITY — normal, but the more the better; spray often.

WATERING — keep the soil moist, especially when actively growing. You can let it dry between thorough waterings in winter.

FEEDING — once a month.

SOIL — mix some pebbles into standard potting soil to be sure the pot drains well.

PROPAGATION — cut off the offsets (small plants) that develop at the base. They will root quite easily if separated when the leaves are at least six inches long.

This plant is easy to grow and can be pretty when cared for, but all too often screwpines look scruffy because their owners are put off by the tooth-edged swords of leaves, so that the plants don't get dusted. Brown tips from overwatering aren't cut off, for the same reason. If you like the shape and color of this plant, try to keep it only while it is young, before it develops the cutting personality of maturity.

Pandanus veitchii

The leaves of these Polynesian plants grow in a spiral around a central core and curve out widely, so the plants need plenty of room. *Pandanus veitchii* has white stripes the length of the leaves. *Pandanus utilis* is completely green with reddish spines on the leaf edges.

A small pandanus fits nicely into a terrarium as a focal plant. A full grown one, however, may be three or four feet tall. Keep a large plant in a somewhat small pot so that it isn't easily overwatered, which damages the tips.

FOLIAGE; EASY; TERRARIUM; OFFICE

PELARGONIUM (Geranium)

LIGHT — east, west, or shielded south.

TEMPERATURE — cool.

HUMIDITY — normal.

WATERING — let the soil dry between thorough waterings unless the nighttime temperature stays high, then water frequently. Don't let water fall on leaves or flowers — they spot.

FEEDING — flowering types: once a month, preferably with a low-nitrogen-content fertilizer to discourage leaf growth. Nonflowering types: regular fertilizer.

SOIL — standard potting soil.

PROPAGATION — root stem cuttings three to six inches long in soil — in spring for winter flowers, in late summer for spring flowers. Remove any eager flower buds until you want the plants to bloom.

Pelargonium hortorum

If you see pretty red flowers growing in pots attached to an outdoor bannister in summer or sitting gaily on a windowsill in winter with no other plants in sight, you can make a fairly safe bet that the flowers are geraniums. Along with ivy and roses, these plants are classics. Their showiness and reliability make them somewhat omnipresent without sacrificing their charm. In flower language, a present of a geranium says "you are foolish." But if you don't tell people that, they'll be glad to receive cuttings or blooming plants.

The name "geranium" should have been preserved for genus *Geranium*, which consists generally of outdoor plants, such as herb Robert. The indoor-thriving geraniums belong to genus *Pelargonium*, from the Cape of Good Hope in South Africa. Some are grown for their abundant flowers and some for their fragrant, attractive foliage.

Most pelargoniums available are varieties of a few species or hybrids created from those few. Among the most popular are varieties of *Pelargonium hortorum*, or *zonale*, which probably acquired that name because the succulent leaves are divided into zones of different tints of green. More important, however, are the long-stemmed heads of red, pink, white, or salmon flowers, which will keep growing for much of the year. Pinch off dead flower heads to encourage longer blossoming. Pinch off leaf shoots, too, to keep the plant bushy and compact.

The plants must be pot-bound, quite severely so, for the best and most constant blossoming. The flower buds don't like heat, so the temperature must be kept on the low side. *Pelargonium zonale* can grow one to three feet tall (try to keep them smaller, though), but miniature varieties are available, some with double flowers.

Pelargonium peltatum has produced many ivy-leaved geraniums in which the beautiful flowers dangle charmingly from baskets along with the attractive glossy leaves. These plants need a higher humidity than other geraniums and should be sprayed daily. Pinch the growth often to keep the plant full. Ivy-leaved geraniums generally bloom in winter.

A third group of geraniums are not grown for their flowers but for their scented leaves. Some of the spicy odors are natural, such as apple, coconut, peppermint, and lemon. Others have been developed with all the care that goes into the making of a great new perfume. Your rooms can smell of almond, lime, roses, pine forests, or even "Old Spice." The foliage is attractive and often tastes good crushed into tea. Try drying some leaves and putting them in drawers with clothing. Some of the specific scent-leaved geraniums are *P. denticulatum* (pine), *P. tomentosum* (peppermint), *P. crispum* (lemon), and *P. graveolens* (roses). They need good drainage in their pots and more frequent watering than the flowering geraniums do.

Geraniums get tired of blossoming (or fragrancing) after months of activity and need a rest. The choice of what you do then is yours. Many people clip off lots of cuttings and start easily grown new plants, throwing the old ones away. Others cut down on water, keep the plants cold (an absolute must!), and cheer mightily when their old friends start to bloom again. With apartment temperatures as they tend to be (high), you're probably better off starting new plants each year.

FOLIAGE; FLOWERING; HANGING

PELLIONIA

LIGHT — east, west, or shielded south; may accept north.

TEMPERATURE — warm.

HUMIDITY — lots; keep on pebble tray and spray daily.

WATERING — keep the soil moist.

FEEDING — once a week with a mild solution.

SOIL — standard potting soil with extra chopped peat added; be sure the pot drains well.

PROPAGATION — root stem cuttings.

Pellionia daveauena

Pellionia doesn't seem to have a common name, nor is it yet a common plant. It is a fairly recent attractive addition to apartment plants from Vietnam.

The distinctive feature of *Pellionia* is the veins on the smallish, oval leaves. *Pellionia pulchra* has greenish leaves highlighted with purplish veins and backs. *Pellonia daveauena* is reversed, having brown leaves and green veins.

The leaves stand up from a creeping stem and are lovely as ground cover in the pot of a tall plant or hanging. In either case, the plant likes its pot and hugs it closely.

Pellionia does well under artificial light and can be used as a charming vine to link separate pots.

FOLIAGE; TERRARIUM; HANGING

PEPEROMIA CAPERATA (Emerald ripple)

PEPEROMIA OBTUSIFOLIA (Pepperface)

PEPEROMIA SANDERSII (Watermelon peperomia, Watermelon begonia)

LIGHT — east or west; try north if that's all you have.

TEMPERATURE — warm.

HUMIDITY — normal, but spray daily.

WATERING — let the soil dry before rewatering thoroughly.

FEEDING — once a month.

SOIL — add sand to standard potting soil or use African violet soil. Be sure the pot drains well.

PROPAGATION — root stem or leaf cuttings in soil. May take several weeks — be patient.

Peperomia caperata

The peperomias (which means "like pepper" — they do belong to the pepper family) fit easily into almost any plant collection. They are small, graceful, and tolerant of most human carelessness, with the exception of overwatering, which makes them rot. There are many species suitable for indoor living. The three I've listed here are reliable and generally available.

I've watched people in plant shops discover emerald ripple (*P. caperata*) for the first time, and almost invariably they say, "How cute!" The small, round leaves are corrugated (rippled) and look like lush dark satin. One of the slower growing peperomias, it is useful in terrariums. It can produce long, white flower spikes that grow several inches above the leaf level. If you don't like them, pinch them off. Some people think they make the foliage even more attractive by contrast.

Peperomia obtusifolia, sometimes called pepperface, has solid, green, waxy leaves. As a ground

Peperomia obtusifolia

Peperomia sandersii

cover, the stems run along the soil surface; as a hanging plant, the thickish stems turn upward of their own accord instead of trailing, because this is basically an erect plant. This *Peperomia* is faster growing than emerald ripple.

I have listed *P. sandersii* as watermelon peperomia. You may find it as watermelon begonia, but there are enough begonias in the world without adding false ones to the list. The leaves of this attractive plant look just like miniature watermelons — oval and green with whitish, stripelike markings.

FOLIAGE; EASY; TERRARIUM

PHILODENDRON BIPENNIFOLIUM
(Fiddleleaf philodendron)

PHILODENDRON HASTATUM
(Elephant's ear)

PHILODENDRON OXYCARDIUM
(Heartleaf, Sweetheart vine, Common philodendron)

LIGHT — any except south in summer.

TEMPERATURE — warm.

HUMIDITY — a little more than normal; spray daily.

WATERING — keep the soil slightly moist; leaves turn yellow if plants are overwatered.

FEEDING — only a couple times a year — they don't need much encouragement.

SOIL — standard potting soil; be sure the pot drains well.

PROPAGATION — root stem cuttings.

Philodendrons are the peasants of the indoor plant set: hardy, reliable, adaptable, and numerous. That isn't to say, however, that you should shun them in your plant collection. They are also attractive,

Philodendron hastatum

versatile, and forbearing — and they grow quickly ~~If you are in need of some ego-building about your~~ ability to make plants grow.

These characteristics explain why philodendrons, especially sweetheart vines, are sold by the thousands, even in dime stores. It's proper to be a snob about dime-store philodendrons; after all, who knows their background or upbringing? Such plants do come in handy if you want to experiment with your techniques of plant care. Normally, though, spend a few pennies more and buy your philodendrons (I keep wanting to say "philodendri") at a plant shop to be sure you get sturdy, disease-free plants that are fully adjusted to apartment living.

Most philodendrons are climbers — in fact, the name means "tree-loving." They, along with many other reliable apartment plants, are members of the arum family from tropical rain forests. Their stems bear aerial roots which help them in climbing. These roots, even if your plants aren't climbing, should be kept moist; be sure to spray them when you spray your plants each day. Please don't decide that the little tannish knobs are dead leaf stems and break them off. They help the plant survive in less than perfect conditions, absorbing moisture from wherever they find it. Philodendrons have smaller below-ground roots than might be supposed from their size, so they can be kept in smallish pots.

Philodendron oxycardium

The most common philodendron, and thus probably the most common indoor plant, is — get this! — the common philodendron. However, it's sometimes called sweetheart vine or heartleaf. It also has two botanical names: the real one is *P. oxycardium* and, the one you'll most likely see in shops, *P. cordatum*. It has small (three to five inches), heart-shaped leaves, and a sturdy vine. It prefers to climb but will be content to hang or lie across a surface. In dish gardens, sweetheart vine is often used to trail around the edge, framing the other plants. Given its head, *P. oxycardium*, like other philodendrons, will put all growing energy into vine-making, so keep it pruned to force full growth. When young (and tiny) it does well in a terrarium.

The fiddleleaf philodendron, *P. bipennifolium* (or *P. panduraeforme*) is one of the large-leaved kinds. The main part of the leaf is an oval, and two rounded lobes grow off one end, making the leaf look rather like a rotund fish. This plant's botanical name is easy to confuse with *P. bipinnatifidium*, the tree philodendron, which has huge (three to four feet long), incised leaves, rather like a giant carrot leaf. It looks like an overgrown mature *Monstera*.

Philodendron hastatum, the elephant's ear, has huge, arrowhead-shaped leaves that can't fail to catch the eye. There is an attractive variegated variety which requires more light than the plain one does.

Many, many species and varieties of *Philodendron* are on the market. They all require approximately the same care and all should have their leaves cleaned regularly to make them sparkle.

FOLIAGE; EASY; TERRARIUM; OFFICE; WATER; HANGING OR CLIMBING

PILEA CADIEREI (Aluminum plant)

PILEA INVOLUCRATA (Pilea, Friendship plant, Panimiga)

PILEA MICROPHYLLA (Artillery plant)

LIGHT — east or west.

TEMPERATURE — warm.

HUMIDITY — lots; keep on pebble tray and spray often.

WATERING — keep the soil moist.

FEEDING — once a month when actively growing.

Pilea cadierei

SOIL — standard potting soil; be sure the pot drains easily.

PROPAGATION — root some stem cuttings.

The three species of *Pilea* described here are all charming, but that's about all they have in common, at least to the layman's eye. They are attractive mainly as foliage plants since the flowers they produce are rather insignificant.

The aluminum plant, *P. cadierei*, is quite startling in the metallic gleam of the pattern of silvery spots between veins on oval, pointed, tooth-edged, green leaves. It is little and tends to stay that way, making it useful in small places, such as terrariums. It may lose some leaves when it starts to rest. If you prune it back, new spring growth will be full and compact.

The friendship plant, originally called the Pan-American friendship plant or panimiga, has plain leaves that are indented and rippled along the veins. Occasional lighter green flowers highlight the brownish-tinged leaves. *Pilea involucrata* also thrives in a terrarium, where its habit of growing shoots straight up keeps it from spreading out of bounds.

The artillery plant, although its tiny, spreading leaves might be likened to shot, actually gets its name from the noise its inconspicuous flowers make when "shooting" out pollen, an action that occurs when the mature flowers are touched or heated by the sun. The charm of *P. microphylla*, however, is in the upright or ground-covering masses of minute, fleshy, light green leaves. The stems grow out in all directions, so regular pinching is needed to keep the plant under control.

FOLIAGE; TERRARIUM

Pilea microphylla

PITTOSPORUM TOBIRA (Pittosporum)

LIGHT — east, west, or protected south.

TEMPERATURE — cool; will not be happy if you

keep your apartment warm.

HUMIDITY — normal; spray frequently.

WATERING — let the soil dry before rewatering thoroughly.

FEEDING — two or three times a year.

SOIL — standard potting soil.

PROPAGATION — root cuttings of young shoots.

Pittosporum is an attractive and sturdy plant that is not too widely grown — probably because of its dislike of too much warmth. But if you, too, prefer cool temperatures, consider sharing your home with this evergreen shrub.

It is grown primarily for its thick, glossy leaves which grow in groups on stems bushing off from a trunklike main stem. Small greenish-white flowers do grow, however, with luck. The clusters of them give off a pleasant scent. It's unlikely that you'll see the berries which follow the flowers on outdoor plants. The seeds in the berries are held together by a sticky fluid, giving the plant its name: *Pittosporum* means "pitch seed."

Prune the growing tips regularly to keep the plant shapely and compact.

FOLIAGE; TERRARIUM (WHEN SMALL)

PLECTRANTHUS AUSTRALIS (Swedish ivy)

LIGHT — east or west. If you have only south-facing windows, keep the plant inside the room out of direct sun.

TEMPERATURE — any.

HUMIDITY — likes it; keep the plant on a pebble tray.

WATERING — keep the soil moist.

FEEDING — once a month, unless you're trying to keep it from taking over your apartment.

SOIL — add vermiculite to standard potting soil;

Pittosporum tobira

Plectranthus australis

loosen surface soil with a fork occasionally.

PROPAGATION — root stem cuttings.

Swedish ivy is neither Swedish nor an ivy. And in most cases, the Latin name tells more than the common. This pretty hanging plant is from Australia. It belongs to the mint family, along with coleus.

Swedish ivy is quite adaptable and so is becoming more and more popular. Its solid green or darkly variegated leaves have scalloped edges and are somewhat succulent. Grown mainly as a foliage plant, it may cooperate and produce tall spikes of delicate, small, white flowers in summer and fall. Pick off the flower stalks after blooming is finished.

FOLIAGE; FLOWERING; WATER; HANGING

PTERIS   (Brake, or table, fern)

LIGHT — any except extremes.

TEMPERATURE — coolish.

Pteris ensiformis

HUMIDITY — lots; keep on pebble tray and spray daily.

WATERING — keep the soil moist.

FEEDING — half-strength solution every other week when actively growing.

SOIL — add sand to standard potting soil. Be sure the pot drains quickly.

PROPAGATION — divide the root clump.

The *Pteris* ferns are among the easier ferns to grow — if any true fern is truly easy. They tolerate changes in conditions better than most, except for sudden drops in the water supply, which makes most plants unhappy.

Unlike most ferns, *Pteris* generally has fronds broken into sections that look, from a distance, like compound leaves. Some fronds are even variegated. *Pteris cretica*, for example, comes in a variety that is lighter green (almost white) close to the stems than at the ends of the leaflets. *Pteris ensiformis* "Victoriae" is silvery striped; it is usually small and fits well into a high-humidity terrarium.

A very popular pteris fern is *P. tremula*, often called Australian bracken. Its leaves are feathery (*Pteris* means "feather" or "wing"), almost carrot-leaf-like, and it spreads widely into an airy-looking plant that needs plenty of room around it.

FOLIAGE; TERRARIUM

RHOEO SPATHACEA
(Moses-in-the-cradle, Boat lily)

Rhoeo spathacea

LIGHT — any except extremes.

TEMPERATURE — any except extremes.

HUMIDITY — normal; would prefer any extra you can provide.

WATERING — keep the soil moist.

FEEDING — once a month.

SOIL — standard potting soil.

PROPAGATION — cut off the little plantlets that develop around the base and plant them; or cut off top and root in water.

This is one of the reliable plants. It survives happily under almost any conditions.

Moses-in-the-cradle (or Moses-in-the-boat, or even -bulrushes, depending on your preference) is another purple plant related to the wandering Jew. But it doesn't wander. It grows upright and shows gray-green tops and purple backs on the thick leaves that overlap in clusters from a thick stem. Boat-shaped bracts cup little white flowers (Moses) through most of the year.

Rhoeo spathacea (also called *R. discolor*) is from Mexico. It often grows outdoors in southern states, where it thrives in coral sand.

FOLIAGE; FLOWERING; EASY

ROSA (Miniature rose)

LIGHT — east, west, or shielded south.

TEMPERATURE — coolish.

HUMIDITY — lots; keep on pebble tray and spray often.

WATERING — keep the soil moist, almost wet.

FEEDING — every two weeks in spring, summer, and fall.

SOIL — standard potting soil; add extra pebbles or bits of pot to the bottom of the pot for excellent drainage.

PROPAGATION — if the plant you buy has only one stem, you can't propagate it; otherwise, divide the root clump.

Rosa

The rose is a dream of a flower that has only infrequently been adapted to the indoors. Legend has it that a pigmy rose was known a couple of hundred years ago, but it disappeared. Then, in the last part of the 1800s, someone discovered one growing on a windowsill of a cottage in Switzerland; the art of growing miniatures stemmed from that discovery.

I said that roses have been only "infrequently" adapted to the indoors. For city-livers, the image of the rose tends to be one of the hybrid beauties that sell for fifteen dollars a dozen. The miniature is a tiny, complete rose bush, thorns and all, reproduced at a height of only four to six inches. The minute blossoms are usually more like those on a wild rambler rose, ragged and brief, than like hothouse bouquet roses. The roses available (not readily, however) are varieties of *Rosa chinensis minima*.

The miniature rose is charming, in spite of its wild-rose-type blossoms, and it draws out the "oh-h-hs" usually reserved for kittens and calendar-picture babies. It does well in windows or under artificial light. The least drop in the water supply turns leaves yellow, so if you go away on a trip, give your rose to a faithful friend to care for. A high-humidity terrarium makes a nice home for a rose if it has a fresh supply of air each day.

Roses tend to grow in exuberant bursts. Prune any branches that destroy the symmetry of your miniature bush.

FLOWERING; TERRARIUM

Saintpaulia ionantha

SAINTPAULIA IONANTHA   (African violet)

LIGHT — east, west, or protected south.

TEMPERATURE — warm.

HUMIDITY — lots; keep on pebble tray and spray air around the plant with lukewarm water.

WATERING — keep the soil moist with warmish water — NEVER use cold water.

FEEDING — every two weeks while blooming; use special African violet fertilizer.

SOIL — African violet mixture. Use pot about one-third the diameter of the leaf spread. Be sure the pot drains well.

PROPAGATION — root leaf-bearing stem cutting in soil or water, or separate double crown (side cluster) of leaves with a sharp knife and pot.

The avid African violet growers have invested the activity with such mysticism that outsiders tend to be a bit afraid to try it. Don't be. The plants are really fairly easy to grow and respond to your care with masses of blossoms.

Saintpaulia is named for the man who discovered the plant in East Africa at the end of the nineteenth century. The simple purple-flowering plant he found has been bred and bred until it now comes in thousands of varieties — flowers of every color, single and double blossoms, and leaves that vary from simple ovals to tortuously curled ruffles. The usually flat bed of leaves serves as a frame for the long-stemmed blossoms.

African violets bloom almost all year. You can make them bloom more abundantly in winter by watering less in summer, forcing a rest period. The stems and leaves are somewhat succulent, so the cutback in watering does no harm unless you let the leaves wilt. Plastic pots hold their water longer than clay pots, so you might do best using plastic for African violets.

Many people grow magnificent African violets in their kitchen windows. They do well there because of the guaranteed high humidity from the sink. If ever you needed a pebble tray, it's with African violets, and although the leaves are hairy, frequent spraying does them nothing but good. Be sure, however, not to use cold water or to spray when the air temperature might drop. Cold of any kind makes the leaves spot.

As African violets get older they tend to develop a single leg that holds the stem cluster above the pot. Repot the plant, adding extra soil to enclose the leg, although changing the soil level isn't recommended for most other plants. Whenever handling the plant, be very gentle; the leaves are quite fragile.

If your apartment doesn't have good light, use artificial lights. African violets might have been invented to show off the benefits of fluorescent or even incandescent lights. And they almost bloom with pleasure at being brought out from under the lights to be admired. They bloom most abundantly if given long days, up to eighteen hours of light each day.

Don't let the extra crowns of leaves develop long on the main plant; they slow the flowering. Cut the crowns off while still small and pot them for more plants. You can, however, leave a couple of crowns on that will make the plant symmetrical. With patience, you'll get a huge mass of flowers on the double or triple plant.

If you buy one of the fancy varieties of *Saintpaulia*, follow the directions that come with it. Fancier plants need fancier care.

FLOWERING; TERRARIUM

Sansevieria trifasciata

SANSEVIERIA (Snake plant, Mother-in-law's tongue)

LIGHT — any.

TEMPERATURE — any, but don't let it get cold in winter.

HUMIDITY — any.

WATERING — let dry thoroughly before rewatering.

FEEDING — every two weeks when growing.

SOIL — standard potting soil. It doesn't even mind terribly having wet toes.

PROPAGATION — any chunk of leaf will eventually root, producing a new plant; or separate the offsets that grow around the base away from the mother plant.

There are few plants more common than *Sansevieria*, and few jokes more common than mother-in-law jokes. But the dignified *Sansevieria* is maligned by its popular name, even if its leaves are sharp and pointed.

When you describe the leaves of this plant you describe the whole plant, because the tall, bladelike leaves grow straight up from the soil. They are basically green with a cream-colored margin. But if you look closely on *S. zeylandica*, you will see gray-green wavy bars crossing the leaves horizontally. *Sansevieria trifasciata* has lengthwise stripes. The leathery leaves grow slowly and probably only one new leaf will appear each year.

Overwatering is about the only thing that will kill the *Sansevieria*. For a plant that's all leaf, brown tips can be very disconcerting.

If *Sansevieria* is grown in sun, it may produce a tall spike of fragrant flowers from the heart of the leaf cluster.

A dwarf species, called *S. hahnii*, can be useful in terrariums when you want something a bit stern to contrast with other, softer foliage.

FOLIAGE; EASY; OFFICE

SAXIFRAGA SARMENTOSA (Strawberry geranium, Strawberry begonia, Mother of thousands)

Saxifraga sarmentosa

LIGHT — east, west, or south (shielded in summer); won't flower well unless it gets some sun.

TEMPERATURE — cool.

HUMIDITY — fairly high; spray daily.

WATERING — keep the soil moist.

FEEDING — once a month; more frequently in summer.

SOIL — add chopped peat to standard potting soil. The pot should be fairly shallow.

PROPAGATION — pin the plantlets that grow on runners into a neighboring pot and let them root before cutting them apart. (They may take up residence in a neighboring pot without any help from you.)

This plant originated in China and Japan and has much of the delicate charm often associated with oriental art. It is, however, sadly misnamed in this country. Called strawberry geranium or begonia, it is not a strawberry though it produces runners as strawberries do; it is not a geranium though its leaves are somewhat geranium-shaped, and it is not a begonia though its leaves are veined similarly to a begonia's. It is, in fact, in the same family as hydrangea, mock orange, and gooseberries. *Saxifraga* means "stone-breaker" from the old belief that some saxifragas broke up gall and kidney stones.

Saxifraga sarmentosa (or *stolonifera*) is a tri-level plant. At the middle level is the low-growing cluster of scallop-edged leaves, which may have white rims. Dangling from the leaf base, and making up the lower level, are hairy, red-stemmed runners bearing miniature plants. (The white-edged variety doesn't produce so many runners as the plain green one does.) The top level consists of fluffs of pinkish-white flowers on tall stems.

FOLIAGE; FLOWERING; EASY; TERRARIUM; HANGING

SCHEFFLERA (or Brassaia) ACTINOPHYLLA
(Australian umbrella tree)

LIGHT — any except extremes.

TEMPERATURE — any except extremes.

HUMIDITY — accepts low but likes its leaves sprayed and washed regularly.

WATERING — let the soil get quite dry before re-watering thoroughly.

FEEDING — three or four times a year. Don't encourage it too much.

SOIL — standard potting soil.

PROPAGATION — root stem cuttings.

Schefflera is a decorator plant. A good-sized one can be quite striking in a living room or office,

Schefflera actinophylla

where it tolerates the usual semineglect. Each group of long, glossy leaves forms an umbrella on the branches growing from the central trunk. The plant looks its best if you keep the leaves clean and shining.

You can buy small umbrella trees (fifteen inches high or so) and have the pleasure of watching them grow — which they do at the rate of about half a foot a year. Or purchase a dramatic "tree" (and pay a dramatic price).

FOLIAGE; OFFICE; WATER (WHEN SMALL)

SCINDAPSUS   (Pothos, Devil's ivy)

LIGHT — any except extremes; shield from direct sun in summer.

TEMPERATURE — warm.

HUMIDITY — normal but spray daily.

WATERING — let the soil get dryish before rewatering. Give it frequent and thorough showers in the sink.

FEEDING — a mild solution every other week.

SOIL — standard potting soil.

PROPAGATION — root stem cuttings.

This plant looks rather like, behaves like, and needs approximately the same care as its relatives, the philodendrons. The leaves of devil's ivy, however, tend to be a bit lighter green and are often mottled or marbled with white. Since the variegation is the main attraction of *Scindapsus* over *Philodendron*, the plant should be kept in lighter places than philodendrons or the leaves turn solid green. The most readily available pothos is *S. aureus* "Marble Queen."

.Pothos will grow in water for long periods of time, but it is most effective when climbing up a bark-covered stake stuck in the soil.

FOLIAGE; EASY; TERRARIUM; WATER; HANGING AND CLIMBING

Scindapsus aureus

SEDUM (Sedum, Stonecrop, Live-forever)

LIGHT — south.

TEMPERATURE — coolish.

HUMIDITY — normal.

WATERING — rarely; let soil dry completely before rewatering. Increase frequency of watering in summer when plant is growing.

FEEDING — once a month when actively growing.

SOIL — add lots of sand to standard potting soil.

PROPAGATION — root stem cuttings (or even broken-off pieces) in sand. You can also divide the root clump when repotting.

Sedum adolphi

The sedums are sitters (*sedere* means "to sit"). They are very popular in rock gardens where they sit low among the rocks, making use of what moisture is available, but not minding a lack of rain. They are succulents, so they hold moisture in their thick leaves and should be treated as you would treat cacti.

Sedums adjust very nicely to indoor life if you learn to ignore them more than you dare ignore thin-leaved plants. But do react quickly if you see that the leaves are limp — they need water. Some sedums have the additional charm of producing quite lovely flowers.

One of the most useful sedums is *S. morganianum*, often called burro's tail. Its plump, tiny leaves grow in ropes up to two or three feet long, which dangle attractively over a basket. The leaves have a silvery-blue tint. Pink or red flowers may grow at the ends of the leaf ropes, but they don't add much to the plant's charm. If you get leaves falling off near the stem base, just cut off the flourishing end and repot it. Be careful where you hang your pot of burro's tail; like all sedums, they are fragile and break easily.

FOLIAGE; EASY; TERRARIUM

SPATHIPHYLLUM (Spathe flower)

LIGHT — any except direct south sun. If you keep it in a dark corner, give it an occasional holiday in brighter light, especially if you want it to flower.

TEMPERATURE — warm.

HUMIDITY — all it can get. Keep it on a pebble tray and spray the leaves daily.

WATERING — keep the soil moist — almost wet — but be sure it doesn't stand in water. The very pointed ends of the leaves turn brown and look ugly.

FEEDING — four or five times a year, especially when active (you can't miss it — new leaves almost pour from the center of the leaf clump).

SOIL — add peat moss to standard potting soil. (Some writers recommend orchid mixture, but I've had excellent results without it.)

PROPAGATION — divide the root clump when repotting.

Spathiphyllum clevelandii

I must admit right away that the spathe flower (much more pleasantly but misleadingly called the peace lily in Britain) was my first apartment plant and is still my favorite. Mine came off the root clump of one my mother has which is more than three feet in diameter (the foliage, not the root). Hers often has a dozen flowers at once and just sparkles with health because nothing crowds it. I have less space so I keep the plant smaller and often display it on a highly polished walnut table. The plant and table seem to reflect each other.

The species of *Spathiphyllum* I'm talking about is *clevelandii*. It has long, pointed, dark green leaves. The white spathe enclosing the small spike flower is the same shape. Your plant shop may carry *S. cannaefolium*. It has broader, lighter-colored leaves and the little flower projection in the spathe is longer. Remove the entire spathe stalk after a flower dies — which may be months.

Don't be startled if you come home some time and your spathiphyllum looks as if it has given up the ghost, with the leaves collapsed around the rim of the pot. Don't start funeral proceedings immediately; the plant just needs a good soaking right away. You'll almost be able to see the leaves rise off their death beds to face another day. Spathes are among the plants that are very happy in plastic pots because the soil stays so moist.

FOLIAGE; FLOWERING; EASY

SYNGONIUM   (Nephthytis, African evergreen)

LIGHT — any except south; will even accept dark corners for a while but the best leaf color comes with some light.

TEMPERATURE — warm.

HUMIDITY — normal but spray regularly.

WATERING — keep the soil moist.

FEEDING — once a month.

SOIL — add some chopped peat to standard potting soil.

PROPAGATION — root stem cuttings bearing aerial roots near the cut.

Syngonium podophyllum

This is the plant with horrible names but an amiability that lets it grow almost anywhere. As you might guess, it's a relative of the hardy philodendron and generally gets about the same care — or lack thereof.

Syngonium (surprisingly easier to say than "nephthytis" although the latter is the name you'll probably find used most often) has an elongating root which gives off twelve- to fifteen-inch stems bearing leaves with three parts, an arrowhead trimmed with a "feather" at each side of the wide section. As the leaves age, the three parts join into a spade shape. The leaves may be solid green, two-tone green, or green and white. They turn yellow if the plant is overwatered or deprived of adequate light. The whole plant can be made to branch by pinching off the growing tips.

It will grow in water instead of soil, but be sure that the root has enough room to grow sideways. The plant will also climb (preferably from a soil base, not water) if encouraged by training it up bark stakes.

FOLIAGE; EASY; OFFICE; WATER; HANGING OR CLIMBING

TOLMIEA MENZIESII (Piggyback, or pickaback, plant, Mother of thousands)

LIGHT — north, east, or west.

TEMPERATURE — cool.

HUMIDITY — normal. Don't spray; the leaves are hairy.

WATERING — keep the soil moist.

FEEDING — once a month.

SOIL — standard potting soil.

PROPAGATION — root stem cuttings with leaves bearing babies.

Tolmiea menziesii

This charming plant is one of the few native North American plants converted to indoor living. It was found in the woods of the Pacific Northwest and was named after a surgeon in the Hudson's Bay Company, which was responsible for exploring the region.

Its delightful nickname of piggyback (or pickaback, depending on your childhood memories) is appropriate because baby leaves perch on grown-up leaves. The little ones stand on short stems growing where the older leaves meet their stems. The leaves are heart-shaped, vaguely reminiscent of a maple leaf, and are light green in color.

Let loose from a confining pot, *Tolmiea* is a ground cover, creeping across the soil by the plantlets taking root. It is related to *Saxifraga* but doesn't have its long runners.

FOLIAGE; EASY; HANGING

TRADESCANTIA FLUMINENSIS (Wandering Jew)

Trandescantia fluminensis

LIGHT — any but direct sun. The leaves are greener and less purple in shade than they are in bright light.

TEMPERATURE — warm.

HUMIDITY — any; likes being sprayed.

WATERING — let the soil get almost dry before rewatering.

FEEDING — it grows like mad even without food, so be very judicious — perhaps a couple of times in spring.

SOIL — add gravel to soil for good drainage.

PROPAGATION — root stem ends; easily done in water.

I'm going to cheat here and talk about two plants of different genera. If you ask for wandering Jew, you are just as likely to get almost identical *Zebrina pendula*. Both it and *Tradescantia* have leaves with striped tops and purple backs. They need the same care. They are different only in that the rather irrelevant little flowers are differently shaped. There is, however, a *Zebrina* variety with bright white stripes on the leaves.

Wandering Jew is one of the easiest plants in the world to grow. It goes everywhere with the least provocation; hence its name. The legend of the wandering Jew says that a shopkeeper in Jerusalem refused to let Jesus rest at his shop on the way to Calvary. The shopkeeper was condemned to wander the earth until Christ's second coming. Several plants with purple foliage and a spreading growth have been called wandering Jews.

The tradescantias are spiderworts often used in botanical research because whole transparent cells are readily visible on the flower stamens. Botanist Edgar Anderson says, "*Tradescantia* is fortunately the kind of plant that not even a botanist can kill. . . ." Neither will you.

The long, hanging stems do tend to get ragged-looking near the pot while flourishing on the ends. So consider just cutting off the healthy ends and rooting them, perhaps once a year. Immortality of a sort.

FOLIAGE; EASY; WATER; HANGING

PLANT NEEDS AND WISHES

PLANTS NEED YOU.

I'm not going to get into the controversy regarding whether plants react to unexpressed hostility or blissful thoughts you may have about them. It is fairly clear, however, that people who talk to their plants seem to have better success than people who don't. Perhaps that is the real meaning of "green thumb" — it's really "green tongue."

The green-tongued people are the ones who, while chattering or expressing sympathy for a dropped leaf, are inspecting their plants daily and acting quickly if they see an embryonic problem. They know each plant intimately and treat it as an individual with distinct needs. They change their care as the seasons change, remembering the plants' outdoor origins. They regard plants as friends who are assisting in their apartment decor, rather than as objects ordered by an interior decorator.

PLANTS NEED CONTROLLED LIGHT

Take careful note of the word "controlled." Light is a good thing only if given in the strength and over the period of time that a plant can utilize it. Otherwise, it can actually destroy.

Light is used by the plant, of course, in the process of photosynthesis, or food making. It can't happen without light. Light activates the chemical process of carbon dioxide (from the air) joining with water (from the soil) to form sugars, yielding oxygen as a waste product. All this happens in the leaves. So, tender loving care of the leaves of a plant is not just to make it more beautiful; it's vital to the plant's very existence.

Most apartment plants originated in heavy tropical growth where they did not obtain light in great abundance. They originally adapted themselves to relatively low light levels, and thus can be harmed by too much light. You'll note that most of these tropical plants have fairly dark green leaves. In general, the darker the leaves of a plant are the more chlorophyll (the magic green substance that absorbs light which sets off the photosynthetic process) they contain. The higher chlorophyll level allows photosynthesis to take place more easily, with less available light. That's why variegated plants require more light than plain green plants do: the variegated leaves contain less chlorophyll.

Low-level light in a tropical jungle, however, does not mean the same thing as low-level light in an apartment. There is no window blocking the sun's rays in tropical forests. Therefore, plants kept on the side of the room away from windows should have slightly brighter vacations once in a while. Move your "dark corner" plants into a north window, or, if possible, your north-light plants into an east or west window for a few days each month. The change gives them a refreshing holiday and lets them tolerate their shaded homes again for a period of time.

On the opposite side of the light coin, however, is the ease with which plants, especially the tropicals, can get too much light in summer. The rays of the sun are very direct through south-facing windows then, and they heat up the air around the plants. Plants react to heat by increasing their rate of photosynthesis and the use of water. Soon the leaves can't cope anymore and they droop; their growth is slowed. The direct rays going through glass can also literally burn the leaves, damage from which they can't recover. You have to cut the brown spots off, and perhaps damage the plant's appearance. Your plants in south windows in late spring and summer need to be shielded from the direct rays of the sun for the four or five hours around noon. You can do this with an almost-closed venetian blind, or more attractively, with a thin curtain.

If you're lucky enough to have a south-facing balcony, regard it as lucky primarily for you, not your plants. Never put your tropical-origin plants outdoors in summer in south sun. They were bred for indoor light, where they are protected by windows. If your balcony faces east or west, however, you can give them a vacation outdoors. Make the change gradually, from indoors to deep shade, to lesser shade, to occasional sun but only if it stays fairly warm all night.

Plants turn the tops of their leaves toward the light source so that the large, flat area receives the light. The tops contain the bulk of the chlorophyll-containing cells. Therefore, you need to turn the pot occasionally so that you can see the leaves and so that the plant won't grow crooked, with all active growth on one side.

PLANTS NEED WATER — IN THE POT AND IN THE AIR

You have probably heard that water is one of the most vital substances on earth. Life evolved in it. Probably only a few bacteria can survive without it, and then only by going into a state of suspended animation.

About eighty-five percent of a plant is water. None of a plant's processes — except dying — can take place without it. A plant without sufficient water cannot even stand upright: the stiffness, or turgor, of a plant's cells is caused by water tension in the cells.

Water in and around a plant is continually on the move. You pour it in the pot. The root hairs absorb it through their thin cell walls, along with minerals dissolved in the water. Stems carry the water upward to the leaves while at the same time carrying food downward from the leaves where it is manufactured. When water reaches the leaves, some of it is used in photosynthesis and some evaporates into the air (transpiration). The evaporation process draws more water up the stem and so the cycle goes on.

The cycle, however, is not a closed one; you must supply water on a regular basis, both to the pot and to the air around most plants.

The immediate urge when confronted by one's first apartment plant is to water, water, water, gaily playing Mistress Mary with the watering can. But it doesn't work. Too much water can destroy a plant about as quickly as too little.

When water sinks into the soil, it clings to the soil particles by surface tension, the same force that makes a glob of water a round drop. The root hairs push their way into the clinging water and absorb it. If there is more water than can cling to the soil and it cannot drain away through a hole in the pot (or into drainage pebbles below the soil), the extra water breaks the watery film on the soil particles and the spaces between particles are filled with water, forcing air out of the pot. Roots then decay and, because leaves survive only to the extent they have roots to nourish them, they turn brown and die, too.

Now you know what happens. How do you prevent it?

You must get to know every plant individually. Some, such as those with large, thin leaves, transpire a great deal. In general, they need frequent watering, with the soil never allowed to dry out. Others, such as the succulents, store water in their leaves. The roots absorb only as much water as can be used by the leaves, so if the soil is kept moist, the water isn't utilized and the roots may rot.

Check each plant daily. It won't need watering

on a nicely convenient schedule. If the air is dry, more water will transpire than if the humidity is high, and more water will be absorbed from the pot.

You have to put your finger in the soil! You may hear lovely suggestions about tapping the pot and hearing it ping when the plant needs water. But the pot doesn't know what kind of plant it contains. Or you may hear of ways to decipher water needs by checking the color of the soil or of the pot, or the temperature of the pot (if the pot feels cool, it still has enough water in it). If you can develop such methods for yourself and find them reliable, fine. But please don't damage the plants just to keep your fingertip clean.

Put your finger in the soil, down at least an inch. The surface dries out before anything else so you can't tell just by touching it. Some plants, however, require regular or occasional drying of the soil. These plants generally have thick roots and need more air in the soil than do plants with thin roots. Thin roots easily shrivel if they get too much air.

I've given a lot of attention to overwatering because it is the most frequent problem. Underwatering can happen, of course. You can easily see the effects. Many plants droop, visible as either a slight limpness or the full drama of a *Spathiphyllum* collapsing around the pot. Water thoroughly right away and they will usually perk up. Some plants such as roses and ferns will often have some leaves turn yellow when they are not getting enough water. Pinch off the yellow leaves and start watering more often.

When you do water any plant water it thoroughly, not with just a dip of the watering pot. There has to be enough water to work its way all the way down through the soil and deep into the root ball so that every tiny, and large, root gets a fresh supply. The best way to be sure this happens is to take the plants to the kitchen sink, pour an amount of water into the pot until it runs out the bottom. When it stops running out, pour in more and let it run through again. When the pot stops dripping, return the plant to its home station. This is what is meant in "The Plant Guide" when it says "be sure the pot drains well": excess water should go quickly through the soil and out the bottom. It must not sit in the pot to rot the roots.

If you don't want to move the plants — or can't — let water run through the pot and into the saucer. Be sure to pour the excess out of the saucer. This involves moving the plants anyway unless you use a basting syringe or sponge to draw the water out.

A few rule-of-thumb generalizations can be made about when plants need less than their usual water supply, but don't accept them as gospel. Know your plants and inspect them daily.

In general, plants need less water:

1. when in low-level light. Photosynthesis is slowed and not much water is used in the process.

2. when plants are in plastic pots. Water doesn't evaporate through the sides as it does through clay pots.

3. when the leaves of the plants are thick. Succulent leaves hold water.

4. when the pots are large. Large pots, of course, hold more water than small ones do.

5. when the temperature of your apartment is being kept fairly low. The rate at which photosynthesis occurs slows in cool air. Also, the humidity of the air increases in relation to a drop in temperature, slowing water loss by transpiration.

6. when the relative humidity is high even if the temperature is high, e.g., when it's raining out.

7. when you have just acquired the plant and it is adjusting to its new environment, or when a plant has just been transplanted. Plants use less water when they are in a state of shock.

8. when plants are in a resting period, especially

before flowering. This sounds rather anthropomorphic, but plants don't see any reason to bloom or start to grow again if they are provided with everything they need.

9. when you are trying to limit the growth of a fast-growing plant, such as philodendron. If no more water than is needed for physiological functioning is available, water won't be used for growth.

Now, back to normal watering and how to handle the excess.

The easiest and safest way is with the wonderful pebble tray, the device that serves two very useful functions at once. Almost every plant will benefit from life on a tray.

A pebble tray is simply a two- or three-inch-deep tray of plastic, fiberglass, or aluminum in which you spread a layer of pebbles or perlite about two inches deep. You stand the pots directly on the pebbles — no saucer needed. You can make the tray decorative, but it should really be plain so that people see the plants, not the tray.

The first purpose it serves is to allow excess water to drain away from the pot into the pebbles below, without your having to do anything more. The other function of the pebble tray is more important. You must play moisture-in-the-air maker for your plants. Most of them need a fairly high level of humidity in the air around them. As has been said, if the air is dry, the leaves will transpire more than if the air is moist. After a while, most plants can't cope with the amount of water that must circulate, and they go limp. Therefore, you have to keep the air around the plants humid, a difficult task in overheated apartments in winter.

After watering plants and letting the excess run into the pebbles, water the tray of pebbles itself, not up to the top, just to within an inch of the top of the pebble layer. Otherwise, the pots may sit in the water, and, the old bugaboo again, the roots may rot. The only apartment plant in this book that glories in sitting in water all the time is *Cyperus*.

Water evaporates from the pebble tray and raises the humidity level around the leaves. If you use hot water to fill the tray, the steam produced is very effective, especially in winter.

The pebble tray itself is not enough in most apartments. You also need to spray the air around most plants as often as you can. You can buy a sprayer for the purpose, or just use an empty atomizer you have handy. Be sure it sprays a fine mist. Use room-temperature water unless the plant guide specifically says to use cold, which can prevent bugs.

Spraying is fun. It gives you an additional chance to converse with your plants and you know you are being helpful. But there are a few "don'ts" about spraying plants: Don't spray right onto the leaves of hairy-leaved plants; they often spot. Don't spray late at night if the temperature in the room will drop much; you might chill the plants. Don't spray when the plants are in direct sun; the water droplets can act as tiny magnifying lenses and burn spots into the leaves. Any other time you have a moment, spray, spray, spray.

About your water supply for both watering and spraying. Unless you know for sure that your town's water supply does not contain a lot of chemicals, let your full watering can and sprayer sit for some hours before watering the plants. Chlorine, particularly, needs to be allowed to escape. Letting the water sit also lets it reach room temperature; some plants, such as African violets, can't stand cold water.

PLANTS NEED TO BE FED — WITH DISCRETION

The sugars produced by photosynthesis are used in building new cells, but they can't do it alone. Certain minerals are needed by plants to build new cell walls.

Outdoors, the supply of minerals in soil is continually replenished by the cycle of life: vegetation and dead animals decompose in soil, releasing minerals for reuse. Indoors, you must supply the minerals.

The packaged standard potting soil that you put your plants in contains a good supply of minerals in the rich compost it is made with. Plants generally won't need more minerals for eight months or a year. Then foliage plants should be lightly fed about once a month during the active period, from about March to October. When resting, they won't use the minerals. Nor will they if they are sick, in low light, or in cool temperatures. All of these conditions slow growth and the plants won't absorb the minerals you add to the soil.

Flowering plants generally need a good supply of minerals from which to construct their blossoms. They should be fed every two or three weeks from the time flower buds first appear until blossoming stops.

The minerals that plants need to be fed most are nitrogen, phosphorus, and potassium. When you see a formula, such as 15-30-15 on a fertilizer container, the numbers refer to the minerals in that order. The numbers are percentages. Nitrogen is used by the plant in building leaves and shoots and in staying green. Phosphorus (or phosphate or phosphoric acid) is used for flowers, fruit, and roots. (Flowering plants generally need more phosphorus than foliage plants do, and the formula should be quite low in nitrogen to encourage flowers rather than leaves.) Potassium (or potash) stiffens plant structures and makes for sturdy growth; it also builds resistance to disease.

The higher number fertilizers, such as 15-30-15, are needed for rapidly growing plants but should be given less frequently. Slow growers — either by nature or because that's the way you want them to be — can use lower-numbered food, such as 5-10-5.

Other minerals, called trace minerals, are also in plant food and do good things, but those are the main three. Once in a great while, however, you may find leaves turning yellow and know that watering is not the problem. Then give the plant a mild dose of an iron product.

Read the directions on the food you buy. Never, never give a stronger dose than the label says. Your plants will probably be better off if you use it both in weaker concentrations and less frequently than the label says. The manufacturers are in the business of selling it, but you needn't give in and buy it often.

Pick a liquid fertilizer that mixes with water or a solid that dissolves quickly in water. Keep your proportions accurate. If the label says one-half teaspoon in a gallon of water and your watering can holds only half a gallon, find a quarter teaspoon measure and use it. Perhaps even more than too much water, too much fertilizer can destroy your plants. Strong chemicals can burn the roots, making the leaves those roots belong to die.

Never pour the fertilizer solution into a pot containing dry soil. Water your plants the day before you feed them so that the soil is moist.

You will probably soon settle on a good general-purpose fertilizer, such as one with low numbers in a 1-2-1 ratio, for example, 5-10-5, which you'll use for most of your plants. If you want to get more particular, you might add small supplies of an acid fertilizer for your citrus plants and perhaps the special African violet mix for, of course, African violets and episcias. Always read the directions carefully. And keep your supplies of all fertilizers small. Plants don't eat much, so there's no point in wasting valuable apartment space on large containers.

The major rule to follow in regard to feeding plants is that if you're in doubt about whether it is time to feed them again or not, don't. And if feed them you must, use a very weak solution.

When light intensity begins to wane in the fall, many plants enter a period of rest. Growth slows, and the plants become relatively inactive. In some plants, the inactivity shows itself only negatively — you suddenly realize there haven't been any new leaves lately. In others, the inactivity is obvious, especially in blooming plants which often become purely foliage plants during winter. (In many, in fact, the whole plant above ground dies, but these plants have been omitted from this book.) The rest period probably evolved because of unfavorable seasons in the native land when the plants' normal needs could not be met. Although the severity of real dormancy has been tempered by the breeding of house plants, many still have at least some need to slow down for a while. Botanists now think that it happens because of the combination of waning light and because there is so much food stored in the plant that the production of growth hormone is slowed or stopped.

Whatever the cause of rest periods, during this time plants need slightly cooler temperatures, less water than usual, and no feeding. Change conditions gradually. Don't lower the temperature by opening the window to let in cool blasts of air. Don't change abruptly from watering every other day to just once a week. Slowly change to an almost dry soil condition, watering just often enough to keep the leaves from shriveling. The plants will still need fairly high humidity levels, so spray them often.

The plants will let you know when to return them to growing conditions, generally by shooting out new leaves.

The rest period is very important to some plants. They seem to need it in order to bloom properly in the spring. *Hoya*, for example, won't bloom unless water is cut way back in winter. *Clivia*, cactus, and crown-of-thorns are some other plants requiring a rest period.

As the year gets well into autumn, keep a close

eye out for signs that some of your plants are beginning to nod off. A few may drop some leaves. Stop all feeding. The plant can't use the fertilizer and it just collects on the pot and soil, perhaps damaging the roots.

As has been said, most apartment plants have had the rest periods almost bred out of them. Read the plant guide carefully for more definite instructions for particular plants.

PLANTS NEED TRIMMING AND PRUNING

It almost breaks your heart to have to trim a plant you've slaved over to get to grow. But, like children, plants need discipline, especially in apartments.

When a bushy plant (as opposed to a single-stem, large-leaved type such as *Dracaena* or *Pandanus*) begins to grow again in late winter, new little shoots appear all over. Left alone, those shoots that make the plant grow tall tend to be the strongest because growth hormone at the top prevents growth on the sides. So some fairly ruthless pinching will be in order to keep the plant from becoming all stem and top.

A pinch is just that, breaking off the growing shoot between fingernails or between nail and ball of a finger. The wounded shoot quickly heals (almost too quickly, sometimes) and growing energy is available to side and bottom shoots that will give the plant a full, compact appearance.

Plants that are being trained up supports should get on with the business of growing long; they should have side shoots pinched off.

The pinching out of young shoots on flowering plants lets the plant use its energy for flowers instead of leaves.

Ivy, *Hoya*, geraniums, miniature roses, wandering Jew, *Impatiens*, and *Cissus* are some plants that benefit from being pinched.

Pinching can be especially important to variegated-leaved plants. If such plants don't get enough light, they produce ancestral plain green leaves.

Pinch out the intruders and put the plant in stronger light so that it reaches all the leaves.

Pruning, on the other hand, is more dramatic. It is the cutting back of whole branches with a knife or shears at a point just above a leaf. It should be done only when active growth is occurring and only to a few branches at a time. Let those cut ones fill out before tackling more. You will probably need to prune only if you let a plant get completely out of hand.

Trailing plants often need cutting back when the leaves nearest the pot turn brown or rot from being in contact with the pot. If you cut back an occasional whole branch, new growth appears at the pot, improving the looks of the whole.

It is often necessary to be quite monsterish in your pinching and pruning. You aren't always doing it just for your own aesthetic benefit. If some plants, such as *Philodendron*, get their stems too tangled, leaves don't get their fair share of light and fresh air. The whole plant takes on a hapless look that doesn't do justice to the care you give it.

Strangely enough, one of the easiest ways to keep plants under control is the one that seems most drastic, pruning the roots. Remember, leaves will grow only if they have roots to support them. Instead of transplanting a plant into a bigger pot just because the plant is pot-bound, try trimming off some roots and returning it to the same pot. Leaf growth will be halted until the roots make a comeback, and you delay the horrid decision to get rid of a dearly beloved green friend before it takes over your apartment.

Remove the plant from the pot when the soil is compacted but not flaking dry. Place the dirt ball on a cutting board. And, using a very sharp knife, cut about an inch away all around. Return it to the pot which has a fresh supply of soil in it. Be sure to tamp the new soil tightly to the old so that the roots won't be stopped by a discontinuity when they are growing anew.

Trim the roots of plants only in the spring or early summer when there will be plenty of time and growing energy for the plant to put out fresh roots. As soon as the plant is repotted, keep it in high humidity (perhaps under a plastic bag) for several days to help it recover from the shock.

A little regular control of your plants is better than a grand gesture once a year. Keep your fingernails in working lengths or carry scissors on your daily inspection tour of your own private jungle.

PLANTS NEED TO BE KEPT CLEAN

One of the aspects of life on earth from which there is no retreat is dust. It settles on floors, furniture, dishes, and plants. Fortunately, the daily spraying of plants also chases away loose dust — another reason for faithful spraying. Hairy-leaved plants or cacti, which can't be sprayed, should be dusted regularly with a soft brush.

The cleaning of plants is not just for the sake of appearance, although that is important, especially on large monsteras or India rubber plants. More vital, however, is the fact that the tiny pores on leaves can become clogged, negating all your regular efforts to keep your plants healthy. The pores, called stomata, are mainly on the back of the leaf but also on the top. They take in carbon dioxide used in photosynthesis and release oxygen as a product. And the leaves give off, or transpire, water from all their surfaces, if they can.

Spraying usually affects only one surface of each leaf, and it is ineffective against the oily grime that accumulates from city air.

Therefore, your plants need real baths every few weeks. Small plants that can be moved without great effort should be taken to the kitchen sink or bathtub. If you can hold the plant upside down with your hand cupped over the soil, you can plunge the whole top into slightly warm, soapy water. Wash behind the ears of each leaf. And don't forget the stems. Rinse the whole plant thoroughly with a spray hose or by dipping it into clean water. Be very careful not to let soap into the soil. Sponge out water that stands in joints where it can cause rot.

Some of your plants will be too big to turn upside down or too fragile to hold without breaking something. On them, use a soapy sponge and wash each leaf completely and gently. Again, rinse carefully.

Those plants that can't be moved need a visiting bath. To be on the safe side, spread plastic around them on the floor before starting to sponge.

If you don't mind sharing your shower with some of your more robust plants, it is safe to turn a gentle, room-temperature shower spray on them. Don't use soap. You get the added benefit that the plants are thoroughly watered at the same time. Be sure the pot has drained before you return it to its home, and dry the plant if its home is in direct sun.

You get a reward for all this effort if it's done on a conscientious basis — lowered possibility of creepy crawly pests that can destroy your plants. Regular bathing will most likely eliminate the eggs of insect pests before they have a chance to develop.

I return now to the beginning: plants need you — a thoughtful, caring you who remembers the needs of each plant and appreciates the beauty that proper care can yield.

PROPAGATING NEW PLANTS FROM OLD

NATURE PROPAGATES MOST PLANTS in a hit or miss fashion that does, fortunately, hit often enough to keep much of Earth green. In your apartment, you need to play mother nature because your plants don't live forever, nor do they duplicate themselves at a gleam in their owner's eye, as schmoos did (if you don't remember them, ask someone about schmoos).

Many plants reproduce by seeds, but it's well nigh impossible to plant one seed of an apartment plant, and it's really a waste of time and space, I think, to get involved with seed boxes, germination periods, and the thinning of seedlings. It's much easier to ask a friend for a cutting from his or her prize specimen. Therefore, I'm not going to talk about planting seeds.

CUTTINGS

Almost every piece of a plant carries within it an amazing ability that in the animal kingdom is found only in a few creatures such as sponges and starfish. It is the ability to produce a whole new organism from a cut section, without getting involved in the complicated rigmarole of sex. I don't suppose most people would envy plants that ability, but it does make the acquisition of new plants simple for you. Such vegetative or asexual propagation yields a plant just like mama without the chanciness of new gene combinations.

A cutting is a piece of a plant that you remove from the plant and encourage to grow into a whole new one. It is usually a top section of stem bearing some leaves or just a leaf itself with some leaf-stem left on. The piece is then put into a medium such as water, soil, or vermiculite, where, with hope and help from you, it gradually develops roots on the submerged end and new stem growth on the top.

Begonias, *Ficus pumila*, and *Pilea* are among the plants in "The Plant Guide" with instructions to root stem cuttings. You'll note that these are usually bushy type plants with thin leaves and slender stems. Select a sturdy stem, preferably near the top but not one bearing a flower bud and, using a sharp knife or razor blade, cleanly cut off a piece about four or five inches long at a point where a leaf grows. Remove that bottom leaf and the one above, but retain several upper leaves.

Many plants such as *Impatiens*, *Plectranthus*, and *Tradescantia*, as well as others that will grow in water, will also root in water. Just place the cutting, also called a slip, in a small container such as a juice glass, which will hold the leaves above room-temperature water while the end of the stem is submerged. You may need to prop up the cutting by inserting it through a hole in a paper cover taped to the glass. A good alternative to a glass is a small, clean medicine bottle with a narrow mouth. Put a small piece of charcoal in the water to keep it clean. You may also want to add to the water some dissolving rooting chemical, such as Transplantone, but most cuttings that root in water will do well without it.

Rooting in water is fun; you can see the root construction as it happens. First, you'll notice that the smooth, cut end develops a thickening, like a callus — which is just what it is. Then, tiny roots will appear at the edges of the callus. These lengthen until, when they are about two inches long, the infant plant is ready to be put in a more permanent home. Water-growing plants can, of course, just be kept in water (see "Plants with Something Extra"), or you can pot them in soil.

The transfer to soil can shock a new water-grown plant for a while as the roots have to adjust to the change in medium. Therefore, most people root cuttings in a medium similar to that in which the plants will later live. However, if you enjoy rooting things in water, as I do, you can help the cutting make the transition. After the roots have developed, add a little soil to the water each day. By the time you almost reach regular soil consistency, the roots will have adjusted and can be transferred without shock.

You can forgo the pleasure of watching roots grow and start right out using a solid medium for rooting cuttings. Fill a small pot or other container with soil or a fifty-fifty mixture of chopped peat moss and perlite, vermiculite, or sand.

Most cuttings will root of their own accord, albeit slowly. You can encourage the development of roots on a cutting in a solid medium, as well as discourage destructive fungus growth, with powders such as Rootone, a synthetic plant hormone that stimulates the rapid production of roots. One container of Rootone will last many years unless you go into the nursery business; however, it's now finally available in small packets.

Dip the cut end of the slip into the powder to a depth of about one-fourth inch deeper than you plan to plant the cutting. Tap off the excess powder. Create a hole in the soil or sand and peat moss. Gently insert the cutting just enough to hold it upright, and press the rooting medium to it.

While rooting, cuttings must be able to carry on the regular business of being plants. Therefore, they need light, water, and humidity. Water the medium the cutting is in — lightly, it doesn't need a full bath. Place it either under artificial lights or in a bright spot that does not get direct sun. You can keep the humidity high by keeping the pot on a pebble tray and spraying often, or place it inside a plastic bag, creating a temporary terrarium. The bag method is often recommended, but I find it dangerous because mold is encouraged in the close, humid atmosphere. Also, you must then gently acclimate the plant to more normal apartment conditions by gradually opening the bag more and more, a slow process.

If you are rooting in soil, you need not check the roots unless after weeks you still do not notice fresh leaf growth (assuming you haven't taken the cutting just before the plant's rest period). A cutting in vermiculite or sand should be ever so gently pulled on after two or three weeks. If it pulls back, clutching roots are forming. Don't tug further; leave the cutting another two weeks before planting the new young thing in its permanent home. If nothing is happening, the cutting will pop out easily. Return it to the rooting medium for another try. If still nothing happens and the cutting is in good shape, you might try making a new clean cut and starting over. Double check that the plant you're trying to root really will develop from a cutting. However, it's unlikely that nothing will have happened if you've taken the cutting during the growing season. Cuttings want to grow if at all possible.

You may occasionally get hold of a slip taken during the plant's resting period. I often do when I visit my family at Christmas. Follow the same procedure, taking particular care never to let the cutting wilt. Eventually your patience will be rewarded and you can celebrate the appearance of long-awaited growth.

African violets, rex begonias, *Sedum*, and *Crassula* are among the plants that will root from leaf cuttings. You'll note that these tend to be plants with some degree of succulence in the leaves. Insert leaf cuttings into a rooting medium at a slant.

They need the same care as stem cuttings. A new tiny plant will grow at the base of the cutting. When the roots are strong and the plant needs a pot, cut away the old parent leaf.

A specialized type of cutting is the rhizome of *Davallia* and certain begonias. A rhizome is an extraordinary underground stem that creeps sideways, producing regular stems and roots. Cut off a rhizome and break it into chunks. Pot the chunks separately and new plants will develop fairly quickly.

PLANTLETS AND OFFSETS

Some plants produce rootless miniatures of themselves on special long stems called runners. *Chlorophytum, Episcia,* and *Saxifraga* are among apartment plants that grow these little plantlets, which are, in fact, much of these plants' charm. A plantlet can be cut off its runner and rooted in water or a solid medium. You can also root the plantlets while they are still attached to the mother plant, if you have room. Place small pots around the big one. Anchor a plantlet in each pot by pushing it slightly into the soil and pinning it down with a hairpin or half a paper clip. The plantlets develop roots and become plants. Clip the apron-string runners and let the new plants lead their own lives.

Offsets are little plants on underground runners, but they already have their own roots. They form at the base of such thick plants as *Sansevieria*, the bromeliads, and *Clivia*. Because they already have roots, all you need do is carefully cut them away from the mother plants. However, all these plants are tough and the cutting is a very messy job unless you wait until the offsets have matured and grown away from mother. Then they just need to be separated and potted by themselves.

DIVIDING THE ROOTS

The propagation of many apartment plants calls for dividing the root clump. Note that this can only be done with plants such as ferns, *Cyperus*, *Maranta*, or *Spathiphyllum* that grow many main stems from the soil. Root division may, quite properly, be regarded as a way of keeping a plant under control (see "Plant Needs and Wishes"), but since it yields two plants from one, I'm including it here.

If you react adversely to the thought of handling roots, you may think this is a horrendous process. It is, however, really quite simple, and often the only way to keep some plants from taking over. You may recall my mentioning my mother's spathiphyllum that is three feet in diameter. She happens to have room for it, but most people in apartments don't. So, at some time in its life, such a plant may need to be divided. It should be done in spring when the plant is vigorous and rarin' to go.

Unpot the overlarge plant, working on lots of newspaper. Remove as much soil (which should be fairly but not dangerously dry) as you can. Put the plant on a breadboard or other hard surface. You may find that the plant seems to fall apart into two or more natural sections. Breathe a sigh of relief and just gently cut through the roots along the natural division. Always cut, never tear. Torn roots don't heal easily.

It's more likely, however, that you'll have to do the whole job yourself. Mentally divide the plant in half. Follow the stems along your mental halfway line down the roots allotted to them. Swallow hard, gather your courage, and make a quick, clean cut through the middle.

Have new, smaller-than-before pots ready. Wrap one plant section in wet paper and plant the other immediately. Then plant the other. Never let the roots dry in the air before replanting, while you hunt up pots.

Keep your two new plants in dim light and water lightly for a couple of weeks. Never water as much as when the plants are healthy — they aren't, and they can't handle much water. And, of course, don't feed them. Keep the plants on a pebble tray; spray often. You are bound to get some dying leaves because some roots will not survive the massacre. Clip those leaves off, and encourage the others.

LAYERING

Layering is the process of making roots grow on an injured stem. It happens because of a plant's tendency to save itself if possible. A simple form occurs if you cut halfway through an *Episcia* or other wandering stem and pin the wounded place into the soil with a hairpin, with the cut held open. New roots quickly grow at the wound, gradually producing another self-sustaining rooted plant, which can be cut away from the mother.

Some plants won't readily produce roots from leaves and they have only a single stem, so that roots can't be divided. But these plants, such as *Dieffenbachia, Dracaena,* and India rubber tree, do tend to get too tall and top-heavy on a stem that has lost its lower leaves. You must take some kind of remedial action. These big plants can't be pinned down as in regular layering. So the wounding and subsequent root growing must be done up on the stem. This is called air-layering, although one of the requirements is that air be kept from the wound so it stays moist — a great example of the occasional absurdity of language.

Air-layering can be either a propagation process, as when a shapely plant is just too tall, or a controlling beautification process, as when the lower leaves have died and the plant is top-heavy. In the former case, you gain two plants. In the latter, you regain one healthy plant with its original charming shape. The process requires real determination on your part because it's impossible to be halfhearted about making a seemingly death-dealing cut in the stem of a single-stemmed plant. You have to *want* to renew the plant and make it beautiful again.

Choose a place on the plant where you want the new roots to be. It may be a couple of inches below the bottom leaves, or, if the plant isn't top-heavy, just too tall, the place can be in the middle. Make a deeply angled cut about one-third to one-half the way through the stem. You must be decisive to make a clean cut but cautious not to cut too far and kill the plant. Firmly prop the cut open with a toothpick or wooden matchstick. It must be held open through the whole development period.

Dust the cut, inside and out, with Rootone or the hormone powder that comes with an inexpensive air-layering kit. Wrap the wound fully with damp sphagnum moss, and then cover the whole moss clump with a piece of heavy, clear plastic. Tape the plastic to the stem at top and bottom of the clump, so that no air can reach the moss to dry it out. Return the plant to its normal position and treat it as you do regularly. Ignore the plastic-coated lump for several weeks. Look, but don't touch.

Some weeks later (it ain't quick but neither was the growth that made the plant too tall), you'll see roots through the plastic. You've done it!

Cut through the stem below the plastic ball. Remove the plastic and quickly pot the new plant in a smallish pot. Give it several weeks in the tight pot, and when you see new leaf growth, transplant into a more usual-sized pot.

The bottom can be thrown away, or, if you're feeling lucky, let it sprout new shoots and see what shaped thing develops. Also, those shoots can sometimes be rooted as cuttings. Or, cut the stem in chunks and lay each chunk on its side buried in a rooting medium. It's worth trying.

Because you live in an apartment, you should think twice before propagating your plants merrily right and left. Do you really want seven hoyas? Can you stand to wash three monsteras? Will your friends accept the care and feeding of the results of your enthusiastic rooting of myriad cuttings?

Be reasonable. Having learned to propagate, don't produce unwanted children.

WHEN YOUR GREEN THUMB TURNS PLANTS BROWN

THE GENUINELY BROWN-THUMBED PERSON has plants that look messy. They don't get a regular bath so the leaves are gummed up and inefficient. Old blossoms are left in place, detracting from the appearance of new ones and even inhibiting their growth. Yellow leaves are also ignored, standing as garish monuments to an I-don't-care attitude.

We know that *your* attitude is fine . . . and yet things occasionally go wrong.

The problem with plant problems is that they're not easily solved. Different causes may produce the same effect, so that you often must go through a trial-and-error process to discover what improves the health of your plants.

The best solution, of course, is not to let plant problems arise. If you give your plants the things they need, including freshly circulating air (which prevents mold), they won't give in readily to incipient problems. Keep all the materials used with your plants, as well as the plants themselves, very clean. It's the old "prevention is better than cure" routine.

Actually, your plant problems are most likely to stem from you — pun fully intended. When buying, choose only absolutely healthy plants. It's no time to feel sorry for the runt with a runny nose; you'll just make your other plants unhappy, too.

Since you can't get down inside the pot to see what's going on in there (except once a year at repotting time or in extreme cases when you just have to inspect the roots), you must take the leaves' word for it that something is right or wrong.

Brown leaf tips is a common problem of apartment plants, and you have caused it. The old bugaboo overwatering. You didn't go back after watering to make sure that the pot isn't sitting in a saucer of water. The soil around the roots is soggy.

Dry the saucer. Let the soil dry until the plant almost wilts. Resolve to never again overwater. Trim the brown part off the leaf tips with scissors. The damaged leaves will sooner or later give up the ghost, but in the meantime, at least they'll be all green.

Almost all plants lose leaves at one time or another, so the sight of one yellow leaf on a bushy plant needn't send you into a frenzy. A succession of them, however, is another matter, one you must ponder.

First, is the plant getting too much water? This is a possibility particularly in pots without drainage holes. Water accumulates around the roots so that they never get any fresh air. Eventually they turn mushy, and leaves turn yellow as a result. They may drop off for the same reason.

However, just the opposite cause can create the same effect. If it's not getting enough water, the plant will divert available water to the growing top, letting the lower leaves die. Water the plant thoroughly and keep it better watered.

On sighting yellowing leaves, assume first that you have overwatered — if the problem is overwatering but you *think* it's underwatering, you'll just compound the problem. You must be patient to see the effect of one approach before trying another one.

Leaves may drop off when the plant isn't getting

enough light. If you have falling leaves — prohibited except on trees in autumn and in songs — check to see how the plant's stems are growing. If they are elongated between leaves, producing a spindly plant, move the plant gradually into stronger light. Let it have a couple of days to adjust at each step of the move before you put it in the bright light you think will cure it.

Too much light is usually demonstrated by the plant wilting easily. There is just not enough water available for all the light-induced activity of the leaves. Like a hostess at the end of a hectic party, the plant wilts.

VITAL POINT — when your thumb turns brown, never rush to feed the plant until you have determined the cause, which is more likely to be water or light conditions than lack of nourishment. A plant that is unhealthy because it needs food doesn't grow, or if it does, the new leaves are stunted. The colors in all the leaves fade a bit and some may turn yellow. That plant is starving; it needs a meal. Give it gruel first: a weak solution, using only half the normal amount of fertilizer. A week later give it a normal strength meal and from then on be sure to feed it regularly. Repotting in new soil when the plant is healthy again will also help.

An overfed plant, one glutted with fertilizer, will usually slowly die because the roots have been burned by the minerals. There isn't much you can do unless you catch the fact right away that you overfed it. Sink the pot in lukewarm water for about thirty seconds. The water should wash the chemicals out before they can do much damage. If fertilizer is not washed out right away, however, accept the fact and discard the plant. I've seen the gradual, sad demise of an overfed Norfolk Island pine, highlighted by mushrooms growing in the pot. Mushrooms do have their own peculiar charm, but they have not yet been admitted to the list of apartment plants.

YELLOWING LEAVES: Soggy soil (let dry, check that the drainage hole is clear); Too little water (be a little more generous); Nutritionless soil (repot and feed faithfully); Insects (inspect the plant carefully and read the next section "Insects"); Drafts (find the calm places around your air conditioner)

BROWN-TIPPED LEAVES. You've let the pot sit in water (trim off damaged tips, resolve to check for and pour out excess water after every watering); Overwatering after soil was too dry (trim and watch it); Needs food (feed or repot)

DROPPING LEAVES: Overwatering (let dry, and take it easy); Too little light (gradually move to a brighter spot); Environmental shock, as when you move a plant to a brighter spot too quickly (slowly does it)

WILTING LEAVES: Underwatering (remember thy plants daily; consider repotting in a wicked, self-watering pot); Too much sun (move the plant)

SPOTS ON LEAVES: Charring from sun after spraying or watering (spray or water only when sun isn't hitting the plant; remove the most spotted leaves if the appearance of the whole plant won't be totally destroyed); Drafts (check all windows, doors, and air conditioners with lit candle and find calm spot for your plants); Too much sun on plants that don't like it (move the plants); Insects (take a good look and treat according to the decision you reach after reading the next section)

FADED LEAVES: Needs nourishment (feed or repot in fresh soil; may need additional iron)

DRY LEAVES: Too low humidity (move plant to pebble tray and spray often)

FEW LEAVES ON NEW STEMS: Too warm and dry (move to cooler room and spray often); Too dark (gradually move to brighter spot)

INSECTS

Plant pests really do not descend on apartment plants very often, especially if you spray and bathe them often. Another way to help prevent them, or to help cure them if you find your plants going buggy, is to hang a product such as No-Pest Strip above each group of massed plants. Its insecticide is very effective within a space of about ten feet by ten feet by ten feet. Another good method of prevention is to isolate a new plant for a couple of weeks to be sure it isn't infested. Talk to it frequently and remind it that if it behaves, it will soon be with new friends.

Even in the best of families, though, you may get creepy crawlies that will harm your plants if you don't locate and destroy them promptly. How do you do this? Inspect your plants every day when you spray them. Take an especially good look at the backs of the leaves and where leaves join stems. These are places that most pests like to congregate. Then, what you *don't* do is grab the pesticide. Pesticides are poisonous and dangerous and not really necessary at all except as a last resort. You have in your kitchen already the most useful of the insecticides — water.

Remove the buggy plant from the others. Take it to the kitchen sink and wash each leaf and stem under a fairly harsh spray of water. A gentle sprinkling does no good. Let the plant dry thoroughly before returning it to the light. You don't need leaf charring in addition to the bugs. Keep the plant isolated and inspect it carefully in a few days. In all likelihood, the bugs will be gone. If not, only then do you get out the insecticide. And if the plant is a duplicate of several in your collection, don't bother. Throw it away.

The major pests that can bug your plants are sucking insects. They suck the juices from leaves or new, young shoots, leaving the plants dejected and lifeless, if not actually dead.

Aphids, also called plant lice, are infamous for

their destruction of garden roses. They are tiny, about a sixteenth to an eighth of an inch long, and usually light green, although they can be brown, black, or reddish. They have long legs and antennae. They are often difficult to decipher against the leaf color, so a quick glance at your plants probably won't reveal them. They, as well as most of the other insects covered here, leave a shiny ooze, called honeydew, on the plants, which helps make their presence known.

A general house plant spray, one recommended by your plant shop, and usually containing rotenone or pyrethrin, will usually get rid of aphids. As with all chemicals, read the label and follow the directions exactly. A more drastic step is to dip the plant (held upside down with soil protected by paper) in a bucket of water and malathion (available at any plant store) mixed with about half a teaspoon of detergent per gallon of water. In case you didn't know, soap makes water wetter, thus helping the chemical do its work. If the plant is a succulent, use nicotine sulfate instead of malathion.

Mealybugs are also plant suckers. You see their eggs as a white fuzz like cotton fluff, along leaf veins, at joints, and even inside flower buds. If the infestation isn't heavy, they will usually succumb to alcohol swabbed with a cotton-tipped stick. If the fluff is everywhere (you haven't been inspecting your plants regularly), wash the plant in the water-malathion-detergent solution.

Scale insects are found most frequently on ferns and palms. On ferns, unfortunately, they look rather like spore cases on the backs of the fronds. Keep in mind, though, that spores grow in regularly occurring patterns. Any hard-shelled, rounded, dark or white lump, especially along leaf veins, that doesn't fit into the spore pattern may be a scale insect housing numerous potentially destructive young. Palms, which don't have spores, may also fall victim to scale, but it is more easily spotted than on ferns. Scales have to be rubbed off with a brush, and they may succumb to the alcohol treatment used with a firm hand. Bathe the plant in the malathion-type insecticide solution if the scale is rampant.

White fly is the biggest nuisance because this sucking insect doesn't nicely stay put waiting to be killed. It flies! Shake the leaves and the little flies zoom off in clouds. Unfortunately, they return to the wingless young which didn't move when they were bothered. You may need several doses of a spray insecticide to get them all. Remember that sprays must, must, must be used at the distance called for in the instructions or the expanding gas of the aerosol can damage tender plant tissues more than the insects themselves would.

Red spider mites, or just mites, are the last of the common pests. They can damage quickly, leaving yellowing spots on curling leaves, so keep a watchful eye for grayish webs on the backs of leaves. The tiny insects (which may be yellow or green instead of red) shake off easily, however, so frequent spraying of your plants drives them out. Give the plants a good, cool bath. If the infestation is very bad (which it usually is if the web is widespread), throw away the plant before the mites infect others. If determined to try, use a special miticide such as kelthane in several doses spaced a week apart. Mites often attack ivy, so keep your ivy clean and the humidity high. Mites, as well as the other pests, thrive in the low humidity of apartments occupied by people who don't really care about their plants.

The main thing to remember in dealing with insecticides is that they are meant to kill. Use with care. When in doubt about a plant pest or its cure, ask at your favorite garden shop. Don't experiment. Silent Spring should not come to your apartment because of your own carelessness in handling chemicals.

There's no reason why your vacation should spell your plants' doom. With a little advance thought, the green inhabitants of your apartment should come through your absence with colors flying — though they will, of course, have missed you.

A four or five days' absence presents no problem if in winter you turn the thermostat down to about sixty-eight degrees or in summer keep the air conditioning going. (If you feel you must turn it off, take your plants elsewhere. They can't stand the heat build-up in your apartment.) Just water the plants well. Make sure all excess has drained harmlessly away. Fill the pebble trays. Wave good-bye.

If you'll be gone a week or more and don't have a kindly, reliable neighbor, you'll need to create temporary terrariums out of plastic bags. This is especially important for small plants that don't hold much water in their comparatively small pots. Water the plants in the usual amount twenty-four hours before you plan to leave. Then just before departure, drop a plastic bag over the head of each plant. You may need to prop the bag up with one or more small sticks or pencils. Tape the bottom of the bag to the pot, and place the pot on a pebble tray where direct sun will not hit. Plants in plastic will stay perky for at least two weeks, often longer. Don't, however, get the idea that they need more water than usual. More water inside the bags than the plants can handle just invites mold to form.

You'll probably have some plants too big to put in small bags. Use large dry-cleaning bags, or place the plants on up-turned pots in the bathtub. Add some water around the lower pots, and tape plastic over the whole tub.

When you return home, don't dash to release the plants from their prisons. Just open the bags and let the plants have a day or so to adjust to the dryer, more normal atmosphere. Then, greet the plants heartily and inspect every inch of them for signs of problems. Make up to them for your absence.

ARTIFICIAL LIGHT TO HELP THE SUN

No PLANT WILL GROW FOREVER in semidarkness, though some, such as *Monstera, Sansevieria, Aspidistra*, and *Syngonium*, can survive for many months. Growth and survival, however, are two quite different processes. You want your plants to grow, within limits.

You may need to augment or replace light from the sun with light from artificial sources, either seasonally or as a permanent arrangement. If your windows look on an airshaft, artificial light may be the only light you can use for growing plants. If small sections of your apartment have no useful function, you may want to brighten those spots with plants under lights. Or, if you have only north-facing windows and want to grow flowering plants, providing an artificial sun is about the only way to do it.

There is nothing mysterious about light, except to the physicists who are still trying to understand it thoroughly. But don't let painful memories of physics classes discourage you. A plant doesn't care whether or not you understand how its life-giving light works, as long as light of the proper intensity is there when needed.

You probably remember from grade-school science that sunlight passing through a prism breaks up into visible component colors of different wavelengths. You may have met that curious individual,

Roy G. Biv (red, orange, yellow, green, blue, indigo, and violet). Other components of sunlight are not visible. Ultraviolet rays, for example, are the invisible wavelengths just shorter than violet. They don't pass through glass.

Infra-red rays, the invisible rays slightly longer than red, can pass through glass, however. And they can damage your plants if they are too strong because they are heat rays — thus the need for breaking south light in summer with a sheer curtain or blinds. (Gamma rays are not light rays in the sense we are discussing them, so their effect on man-in-the-moon marigolds need not be considered.)

Plants actually use only the visible (Roy G. Biv) portion of light. The chlorophyll in plants absorbs the red and blue rays of the spectrum and uses them in the complex carbon-fixing process of photosynthesis. The middle, or green, portion of the spectrum is reflected by plants, making them look green. You don't need the whole spectacular range of sunlight to gratify your plants. Artificial lights that produce red and blue rays will do the job.

LIGHTS AND THEIR ARRANGEMENTS

There are four major types of lighting you can select from: incandescent alone, fluorescent alone, the two in combination, and special plant-growth lights.

For many years, the only artificial lights available were the incandescent (meaning "glowing with light from heat") bulbs invented by Thomas Edison. Most of the lights in your apartment are incandescent. They can be very satisfactory as lights to supplement daylight. You can, for example, place plants on an end table under a lamp and extend the plants' day, a cheerful sight on a winter night. You can even buy lamp stands containing brackets to hold pots.

Incandescent bulbs have one characteristic that is both good and bad: they give off light mostly in the red range, which is associated with heat. Red rays encourage flowering of plants but the associated heat can damage them, so the plants must not be very close to the bulb and air must circulate around the lamp to carry away the heat.

I have successfully made miniature roses bloom on an end table under a tall lamp containing a 150-watt bulb. The plant was never closer than eighteen inches to the bulb and the temperature never reached above about seventy-six degrees under the light — not too warm for a warmth-loving plant. Not all the light — or heat — of an incandescent bulb, of course, is directed downward. Much goes upward or even outward if the shade around it is not opaque.

If you try this pretty arrangement, choose small, warmth-loving plants such as roses, African violets, pilea, young ferns, or episcia. Keep a close watch on the temperature and the soil moisture.

The lights in modern offices are generally the newer fluorescent tubes, in which a chemical coating inside a vapor-filled tube is excited by electricity into glowing, or fluorescing. These tubes don't give off much heat, but the light they produce is harsh and sometimes irritating to people's eyes.

Fluorescent tubes give off light mostly in the blue range. In fact, they are cool specifically because they don't give off much red light. Blue rays encourage strong stems and leaves and help regulate respiration of the leaves. Any fluorescent light is useful as a supplementary light to extend the day, or even as full-time light by which dimness-tolerant foliage plants can hold their own in dark corners.

If you want to grow a variety of plants under artificial lights only, however, you will need *balanced* lighting. For many years, people have combined incandescent and fluorescent — the former for flowering and the latter for strong, full leaf growth. If you want to combine the two, remember the ratio three to one. For every three watts of fluorescent, use one of incandescent, for example, two forty-watt fluorescent tubes and one twenty-five-watt bulb. That ratio is the product of a great deal of research by the Department of Agriculture and the lighting industry. The proportionately small amount of incandescent is enough to encourage flowering without giving off so much heat as to be harmful. If you decide to go in for artificial lights in a big way and have a long table you want to illuminate so that you are using ninety-watt tubes, use two or three twenty-five-watt bulbs instead of one sixty or seventy-five, so that the heat is not concentrated.

Fluorescent tubes, however, now come in great variety. They are classified as daylight, white, cool white, warm white, and natural. Those words are printed on the tubes. The best for plants are the daylight and cool white lights. The former provides mainly blue light, the latter has been strengthened in the red range. One of each in a two-tube reflector unit provides the balanced light needed for strong plant growth.

A simpler but more expensive way to get balanced light is to choose one of the several types of plant-growth lights produced by Westinghouse, Sylvania, General Electric, and others. These tubes have been created to give off strong red and blue rays for plant growth. However, the purplish glow they emit is not terribly attractive in a living room. Also, the tubes cost three dollars each or more, depending on the size, and they are not available at every hardware or drug store, a difficulty the plants won't appreciate if their artificial suns burn out on a weekend.

If you decide to go the special light route, consider the new wide-spectrum tubes, such as Vitalite. They almost duplicate the sun's light, including some ultraviolet rays, which seem to help cacti and are not available to plants behind windows.

The light given off by these wide-spectrum tubes is quite like natural sunlight and is easy on the eyes.

Regardless of the kind of lights you select (except for incandescent which are not practical for more than one or two plants at a time) you need to illuminate completely all the plants that you want to reach. A shelf four feet long should have a four-foot fixture hung over it. Plants that need the most light should be placed in the center directly under the tubes; lesser-light lovers can go along the edges and ends. In general, apartment plants need about fifteen watts for every square foot of surface area.

Ready-made plant growth fixtures are available. They cost from eighteen dollars up . . . and up. One simple and inexpensive type consists of a two-tube metal reflector which hangs from the ceiling by a chain. The chain can be raised or lowered as needed; just hang it over whatever shelf or surface you select. The most common size of this type of unit is four feet long and holds two forty-watt tubes. It has the disadvantage of being overwhelmingly functional looking.

A slightly more decorative unit has the reflector mounted on legs so that it can be moved up or down. This type is ofen found in shorter lengths for use in small places and comes with a built-in tray to hold the plants. It has the advantage of being relocated easily. Units containing a socket for an incandescent bulb as well as the tubes are also available from gardening catalogs.

The units are adjustable because plants come in different sizes — and they grow. Raise the smaller plants on overturned pots or on raisers of your own invention, so that their tops are on the same level as the taller plants. Position the lights about six or seven inches above the leaves. If the lights are twelve inches or more above the plants, they probably won't gain any benefit. In fact, they will end up looking scraggly because stems will grow to reach the light but leaf growth won't keep pace.

If the lights are too close, the leaves may curl up. Also, there is a chance that the plants will grow against the tubes; even the nonhot fluorescent tubes can damage delicate plant tissues by contact. You won't be able to get at the plants to pinch off overexuberant growth if the lights are too close. Most plants for small places should be kept fairly small. If you must err in calculating light distance, however, err on the closer side for greater intensity.

If lights are being used to supplement natural light on short winter days, four or five hours in the evening is sufficient. If they are the only source of light for the plants, about fourteen to sixteen hours a day is needed. Both uses should have the suggested fifteen watts per square foot. Until lately, the rule has been never to leave the lights on twenty-four hours a day because plants, it seemed, needed darkness to recover from the day's activities. However, commercial artificial light gardeners have been experimenting, and early evidence indicates that perhaps some plants don't need a period of darkness after all. You might want to experiment on your own with African violets or other flowering plants.

You can depend on your own firm-mindedness and turn the lights on and off yourself. It's safer, however, especially if you travel or go away on weekends, to invest in a simple timing mechanism that turns the lights on and off at a set schedule. Whichever method you use, the timing should be the same every day. Don't keep the plants in a state of perpetual suspense by giving them ten hours of light one day and nineteen the next. Plants, again like people, develop a rhythm to their day-night activities, and once you, playing sungod, have established that rhythm, the plants are healthier if you stick to it.

For foliage plants, it doesn't really matter whether you use ten hours a day or nineteen — so long as it's the same every day. But some flowering plants are known as "long-day" plants. They won't bloom abundantly unless given long days and short nights. (It's that bit of knowledge that allows florists to force flowering plants to bloom out of season.) Your African violets will flower best if they are given eighteen-hour days. (If you're an eight-hour-a-night sleeper, buy a timer.) Begonias and other flowering plants in this book don't seem to mind how long their day is.

If your apartment gets enough natural light in summer to let you turn off the electric lights, do so. Just don't forget the plants in dark corners; move them near windows. And if a window faces north in winter, it will most likely still face north in summer, so you'll have to remember to provide the extra lamp light, especially if you're aiming for nice summer blossoms.

CARE OF PLANTS UNDER LIGHTS

Remember from an earlier chapter — the more light a plant has, the more water it will need. Be prepared to check the soil moisture of plants under lights every day, even if you aren't so careful with your other plants. Tubes may not give off much heat, but what they do give off dries the air. Keep all the plants on pebble trays that you water regularly. And spray the plants that can take it (the nonhairy ones) daily. Self-watering plastic pots are especially helpful under lights.

Even under lights, plants have temperature preferences because, of course, the lights are turned off at night. Keep those plants that like cool nights together, perhaps by an outer wall. Warmth-loving plants will do well by an inner wall or in a room where you don't turn the thermostat down.

Plants that get a lot of light are going to grow. That's why you have them under lights. Therefore, they are going to need faithful feeding so they have the minerals to serve as cellular building blocks. Feed them every other watering with food half the strength called for on the fertilizer package.

Growing plants need more frequent trimming

than usual. And if you remove the extra-nice plants from their illuminated womb to display them occasionally, make sure you don't subject them to the shock of drafts.

You are dealing with electricity in a place where you use water, a potentially dangerous situation. Be careful. Put water only where you want it to be — in the pots or in the pebble tray.

The lights are on for a long time. Be sure that all the fixtures, especially if you use the heat-making incandescent bulbs, are covered in asbestos or are made of ceramic.

Lights that are on for a long time every day are good for plants, but not for a colorful oriental rug or a nearby chintz chair. Install your lighting system where it won't fade colors in furniture or rugs.

Fluorescent tubes go dim gradually, unlike incandescent, which die without warning, usually when you least expect it. Replace tubes regularly, about every six months or so, before they start to turn gray at the ends. There is a great difference in the intensity of old tubes and new ones, which can shock the plants.

You've probably noticed that many of the plants you buy at garden shops are planted in mixtures of moss, vermiculite, and/or perlite instead of soil. These plants were probably started under artificial light.

Many indoor gardeners use only such soilless mixtures for plants under lights because potting soil dries out so quickly. If you're going in for gardening with lights in a big way, you'll probably do well to switch completely to soilless material. But if you use lights for a supplement or for a few special plants that you wouldn't be able to grow otherwise, don't bother. Apartments are generally too small to clutter up cupboards with more mixtures than absolutely needed. This is another area for your own experimentation.

CONSIDER THESE IDEAS

One of the times in plant-tending when it's easy to be impatient is when rooting cuttings for new plants. Some cuttings don't cooperate well if you take them at the wrong time of year. They may sit there wilting glumly, waiting until the year is right before they root. Or worse yet, they rot in a dramatic show of disapproval. It was this slowness to react that caused some people to root cuttings in dim light where they wouldn't wilt so easily.

But you can fool them and have new plants growing very quickly just by putting the stem cuttings in water under a light — an end-table incandescent sixty-watt bulb will be enough. By quickly, I mean only a few days.

The light they receive makes young roots very strong, so you should not have any trouble transferring the plant to soil when the roots are established and about two inches long. In fact, artificial light is better for rooting cuttings than strong sunlight because it is even and less apt to be scorchingly hot than sunlight. As with all propagation, be sure to keep the humidity high.

Now back to grown-up plants.

You want to put a large plant in a corner, but there isn't enough light. Install a spotlight fixture on the ceiling above the plant. Use a 130-volt incandescent light instead of the usual 120-volt. It gives off less heat. Position the plant about four or five feet below the spotlight.

Attach lights under a bookcase shelf and put plants on the next shelf down. You can use a metal reflector or paint white the underside of the shelf the lights are on. You'll probably want to build a shield a couple of inches down from the shelf to protect your eyes from glare.

In the kitchen, attach a light unit under a wall cabinet. You can have lovely flowers on the counter while you cook and clean up. They'll love the humidity, too.

Hang a plant basket from the ceiling so that the basket is suspended below a wall light or ceiling light containing 130-volt bulbs. Remember, incandescent was around before fluorescent and you can grow some lovely plants in such light.

Use supplementary lights on foliage plants even if you have adequate light from windows. Your jade plant may bloom. Leaves of all plants get healthier looking. Coleus, for example, will develop colors that are almost neonlike in their brightness.

If you are trying to create a special effect with ivy, such as trailing it around a window, the ivy will grow faster and complete your scene more quickly if encouraged by artificial light.

You've bought a small replacement plant of, say, a fern but miss your big old one which up and died? Urge the new plant with a regular dose of indoor lights.

Consider brightening a dark corner with an artificially lighted terrarium. You'll see the plants clearly and your choice of terrarium inhabitants will be wider than if you depend on window light. Be sure that air can circulate in the terrarium.

Look for surprises if you use artificial lights.

One of the joys of gardening, even on an apartment scale, is that in spite of this book and others like it, there are really few hard and fast rules. Plants are living creatures with their own individual modes of living — or dying. So what works well for you is right for you. Experiment with lights to assist the sun in your own way.

PLANTS WITH SOMETHING EXTRA

ONCE YOU'VE DISCOVERED that there are plants you can grow in the conditions prevailing in your apartment, you may get a yearning to start playing handicrafts with the plants. Take advantage of their natural proclivities to help you decorate.

THE RESTLESS PLANTS — CLIMBERS AND TRAILERS

The time for a new approach to your plants may come when you move into an apartment with a dinette off the living room and you want something visually pleasing to divide the space. A living curtain of plants can do the job with more flare than most bamboo screens. Or the time for a change may be forced on you when your cat discovers the sheer joy of eating a spider plant and you need to get the plant out of reach. (I have yet to find the reason for cats' tastes for spider plants.)

Certain plants are quite willing to cooperate in your search for something new. They climb enthusiastically. They cascade appealingly, seeming to defy the usual plant's need to grow upward. I call these plants the restless ones. They are at their best when given something more to do than just sitting in a pot on a table. In "The Plant Guide," they are described as "hanging," "climbing," or both.

Hanging plants can, in general, be defined as any plant whose stems droop. A small Boston fern will grow nicely on a table in a normal pot . . . for a while. When it gets larger, however, its stems droop until the long fronds reach below the level of the pot bottom. Then contact with the table damages the fronds. Other plants, such as *Sedum morganianum* and *Columnea*, don't arch upward before drooping; they just fall straight down from the pot.

Pots, or baskets, as hanging pots are usually called, aren't going to obligingly sit in midair without support, unless you've learned the power of levitation. So you have three main types of container to choose from: those that extend from the floor, from a wall, or from the ceiling.

The pedestal type, such as fern stands, stand on the floor. They are often of wrought iron and may be quite ornate. Don't choose a stand that has so much character of its own that it detracts from your plants. Pedestals may come with one pot holder, two, three, or even more. Floor-to-ceiling poles have several holders, at different levels. The holders may be rings into which the pot is slipped. This kind requires that you use only one pot size. Others have holders like saucers in which you can rest pots of various sizes.

Wall baskets may have a flat side that fastens to the wall. Plants for this type must be danglers, which can hang over only one side of the container. *Episcia*, *Hoya*, or *Ceropegia* will go well in such a basket.

Other wall brackets have the ring which holds the pot extended on an arm, a foot or so away from the wall. Spider plants, ferns, *Tolmiea*, and begonias generally need this type because stem growth occurs all around a 360-degree circle. Be sure that the wall you fasten these brackets to is sturdy enough to bear the combination weight of pot, soil, and plant.

Probably the most effective use of hanging plants is in baskets suspended from the ceiling. Such baskets are available in every form, from simple plastic pots, with permanent saucer and chains attached, to ornate bird cages through which plants tumble from shallow pots. Any attractive container to which you can fasten chains or strong cords will serve as a plant basket. Again, be sure your ceiling can support the weight.

Wall brackets can also hold the chains of a basket, combining two methods of support. These look lovely with the bracket fastened above a window so that the basket hangs in the sunlight at about eye level.

Hanging plants need all the normal care and selection of location by light and temperature that all plants do. One of the biggest problems, however, can be watering the plants without dribbling all over your furniture, unless you live in a plastic paradise.

The simplest solution is to use only baskets into which removable pots fit. The pots can be taken out, the plants watered thoroughly in the kitchen and let sit while excess water runs out, and then returned to the basket. If the baskets are solid and contain pebbles or perlite for the pot to rest on, the plant can, of course, be watered in the regular way, *in situ*. This is a must if the plants are tangly and will break if pulled through the chains. Plastic pots without drainage holes are useful in hanging containers, both because they are light in weight and because they don't drip. Be sure to regulate your watering: plants in plastic pots need less water than plants in clay pots do.

Plants that hang in isolated glory in baskets need more water than plants in groups on tables. They lack the humidity of grouping and air circulates freely around them, evaporating the water quickly. Choose a watering method you can live with comfortably. To be effective, hanging plants must always be healthy. Be sure to spray them daily or even oftener.

Don't be attracted by the ornate openwork baskets in which sphagnum moss serves as the pot. They are intended only for outdoor use where drips don't matter.

You needn't bother with special stands, brackets, or baskets to display hanging plants. Smallish ones, such as *Fittonia* or *Pilea*, can be very attractive if just set on an upturned pot among other plants so that it is raised to a higher level. This method has the advantage that the raised plant still gets moisture from surrounding plants. Also, the hanging vine tends to tie the group of plants together visually. Trailing vines, such as wandering Jew, do nicely this way. Just be sure that the other plants don't have their light blocked out.

Many vines have just as strong an inclination to climb as to trail. But they need something to climb on, chosen according to how they climb. *Cissus*, for example, shoots out twining tendrils that wrap around a thin bamboo stake or a cord. *Philodendron* and *Ficus*, on the other hand, give off rootlets that cling to rough surfaces. They will climb a bark-covered stake or rough driftwood. Ivy, of course, can attach itself to a brick wall. None of the climbing plants is going to leap gaily up the support the minute you provide it. So you must think ahead, decide what you want months or even a year or more from now, and be patient.

The simplest support is a stake driven carefully (there are roots in there) into the soil. A smooth stick will do, or you can get bark-covered ones at plant shops. Many plants, not just climbers, need this kind of support when they get taller than their fragile stems can bear. *Impatiens*, for example, usually needs to be tied to a support if it gets more than about fifteen inches tall.

When working with climbers, you must give the plant a clue as to what you want it to do by tying a growing tip to the stake as high as it will comfortably reach. When it grows a few more inches and begins to dangle downward, tie it again. When it reaches the top of the stake, trail it down, and then up again. Eventually, you'll have a full-looking but compact plant which is, actually, one long vine.

This same principle can be used with fairly

ornate wicker trellises which look like ladders, fans, hearts, or any shape you want. Remember never to force the vine. Force can break fragile stems. Just give it guidance by tying it loosely.

Real patience is required for growing plants up a cord until they reach the ceiling. But they can be beautiful and well worth the wait.

Add the cord when repotting a twining plant, by inserting a long, preferably green or black, cord down through the soil, well anchored in pebbles or even glued to the base of the pot. Place the plant where you want it, perhaps on the floor at the side of a window. Lead the cord to the ceiling and fasten it with an eye-hook screw; make sure there is no slack in the cord. When giving the plant its daily humidifying, be sure to spray the cord, too. This water-holding capacity of the cord is why it's better to use than wire.

Several pots evenly spaced across the floor with strings to the ceiling make up an incipient room divider. Or, if you don't find any appeal in strings, you can use a bamboo or plywood grill-type room divider which will look all right while the plants are making their way upward. If you use this arrangement, be sure the divider will not warp with the frequent spraying the plants will need.

Plants that are supposed to climb will need regular pinching off of side shoots so that all the growing energy is used for elongating the vine. If you want the total effect to be thick, root the shoots you cut off in the pot with the mother plants and start whole families growing up the same support.

In modern apartment buildings, the chances are not good that you'll have a window right next to where you want an animated room divider. Or even if you do have a window, you won't want the plants to turn their backs on you to face the window. So install fluorescent lights or Cool Beam floodlights above the plants (see "Artificial Light to Help the Sun"). The plants will grow faster and be more attractive.

Even if you have all the plant growing space you want (and if you do, I don't believe you live in an apartment), the addition of hanging or climbing plants to your collection contributes a liveliness that pots sitting by themselves lack. Bernice Brilmeyer in *All About Vines and Hanging Plants* seizes on the contribution that vines make: "Vines are mobile, not static; exuberant, not depressing; in tune with today's vitality and restlessness, yet somehow soothing, too."

PLANTS THAT SWIM

There are a lot of cuttings that you can root in water before transferring them to a pot. Some of them, though, such as nephthytis, ivy, wandering Jew, crotons, and *Cyperus*, need not be transferred. They will keep on growing very attractively in water. Plants in "The Plant Guide" that will do well in water are designated "water" in that chapter and on the chart at the back of the book.

It seems odd that plants will grow in water considering the number of times plant care instructions specify "be sure the pot drains well." The difference is in that life-giving gas, oxygen. Oxygen around the roots of a plant in soil is driven out by excess water, but there is plenty of oxygen for the roots of a plant sitting just in water, and the supply is constantly replenished from the air. Think of how healthy the plants in a well-balanced aquarium stay.

My cat and a philodendron that lives anchored by colored marbles in a glass brick have established a wonderful rapport. As far as I know, the cat doesn't drink any water except what she laps from the watery home of the plant. And she hasn't turned green yet. It does mean, however, that the plant needs fresh water every day. Both plant and cat are thriving.

You can use almost any kind of container for water-living plants — clear glass vase, low ornate bowl, or, if you're hung up on pop art, a tomato soup can, but be sure to spray it inside with a clear plastic to keep it from rusting.

A plant with long stems, such as nephthytis, or aglaonema, could just stand in a tall vase, but if the leaves start to dangle, their weight may pull the plant out. Therefore, it's safer to anchor all swimming plants into their container. Marbles, aquarium gravel, pretty, well-washed beach pebbles, white sand, or whatever you can find that won't react with the water will serve as an anchor when spread over the plant's roots. You can also gently press the roots onto one of the prickly frogs used for cut flowers, but be sure to feed the plant in its first water supply to minimize the shock of injured roots.

Actually, all plants in water need feeding just as if they were in soil — more so, in fact, because there are no nutrients in water. About once a month, use a weak fertilizer solution (preferably not a blue one) instead of plain water to replenish the supply. Also about once a month, you'll need to clean the bowl of food that has dried on the sides. You might combine these operations. At other times, just add water to replace that which has been used or evaporated.

Some aquarium-type charcoal should be mixed with the anchoring pebbles to keep the water sweet. Wash it off first to be sure coal dust doesn't dirty the water. If you don't like the look of charcoal in a clear container, omit it, but be sure to change the water completely at least once a week.

When putting in water for any purpose, pour it only from a supply which was taken from the tap hours or a day before. The chlorine will have had a chance to escape and the water will have warmed to room temperature.

Keep swimming plants in a fairly warm spot so that the temperature of the water won't drop much at night and shock the plants.

After some months, some of your plants growing in water may begin to droop and look less than perfect. If this happens, remove them from their watery home and plant them in soil for a refreshing vacation. You can return them to water later if you want, or just root a piece in water and start all over.

If you want a really special look, and you're tired of your highly successful — or perhaps not so very successful — terrarium, clean the glass container thoroughly and convert it into a pond containing several different water-loving plants. It won't work too well in a narrow-necked bottle (too difficult to change the water), but it certainly will in a wide-mouthed bowl or square terrarium. A selection of plants resting in a bed of colored stones or marbles will call attention to themselves in a way that plants in clay pots often don't.

And next thing you know you may be going in for real aquariums. Fishes are nice, too.

WINDOW GARDENS

You have a limited amount of space and can't afford to "waste" a table on plants? You have a picture window with so blank a look that your room always has a startled appearance? You just like plants and want to use them to their best advantage?

A window garden may be your answer.

The first thought in planning a glorious window garden is to use the window sill. But the apartment with sills more than a inch or so wide is a rarity these days. So what are your alternatives?

First, you can create new sills — several of them — by using the old-fashioned but still effective glass shelves. Fasten bracket strips to each side of the window, attach holders where you want them (some can be screwed to the wall directly), and lay the glass shelves across the holders.

You could, of course, do this with wooden shelves but plants on the lower shelves would receive a great deal less light than they do with glass shelves.

Use your own artistic and plant sense to select which plants to put on the shelves — based on what direction the window is facing and how cold it gets at night. If the window faces south, be sure to use a venetian blind or curtain over the window so that you can control just how much light the plants get.

You might consider tying the whole effect together (not quite literally) with a dangling vine that reaches down several shelves. Or train the vine around the whole window so that it serves as a frame for flowering plants.

If you don't want your whole window blocked with plants, there are a couple of ways to create interesting displays at sill level — a window box or a platform.

The window boxes of European fame have moved indoors into apartments with ease but with some modifications. The original boxes were intended for outdoor use, and they dripped. The indoor boxes are troughs (which, actually, can be used anywhere) that have been lined to prevent dripping. Most troughs, however, are low. When used by a window they must be raised to window level for the plants to benefit from the sun.

You can fasten a plastic or fiberglass box to a window if the frame will safely bear the weight of pebbles or perlite for drainage and the dirt-filled pots. Don't try to fill the box with dirt and plant things in it. The weight of all that soil will probably be overwhelming, and you'll have too much messy digging to do when plants need changing. It's easier all around to put pots resting on a layer of pebbles in the box. You can hide the pots with a wandering vine or peat moss, which holds moisture, thus raising the humidity level.

Planter boxes are also available on legs that raise the box to the height of an average window sill. These are usually of metal and may be mounted on wheels, in which case you can just roll them into the kitchen for watering and bathing the plants.

Most such legged planters are not wide enough for more than one row of pots. If you want a really massive display of plants at the window — sort of a miniature jungle — you might construct a plant platform which juts out from the wall at sill level. This platform is just a wide board (perhaps a large breadboard) fastened to the wall by hinges. The hinges allow it to be folded downward, out of sight, when not in use. Two hinged triangular braces or two hinged wooden or metal right-angles having legs that reach the floor (such as are on gateleg tables) will provide the support needed for the platform.

Then let your imagination take over. A water-filled pebble tray the size of the board will humidify the air, allowing you to mass plants in a jungle effect. Or you can keep the plants on their individual pebble-filled or empty saucers, depending on the requirements of each plant. Place some cut flowers among the potted green foliage plants.

One of the great advantages of such a platform is that you can use it as a sunlight camp for flowering plants while you wait for them to peak. Then move the bloomers out to a coffee table where they can be admired on their own.

However you arrange a window garden, be sure not to let small plants get lost among larger ones, unlighted and unloved. Keep the larger ones under control with regular pruning, and turn all plants regularly so they will grow evenly. Keep a close eye out for insects or other pests and quickly remove from the group any plant that looks in danger.

TERRARIUMS

IT'S RATHER DIFFICULT for modern cliff dwellers without a balcony to have greenhouses, and many apartment managers won't allow them there. Small, window-type greenhouses, however, are now commercially available.

You can have a greenhouse-in-miniature by constructing a terrarium. "Aquarium" means water habitat, so "terrarium" — if you remember your Latin — must mean land habitat. (It is nice to have language be logical once in a while.)

Terrariums are sometimes called bottle gardens, but they don't require a bottle. Any almost-closable clear glass or plastic container will do. Since leaves are falling in colorful array as I write this, my first thought is a gallon apple cider jug. Just be sure that the mouth is at least an inch in diameter; it can be difficult enough to get an ornery plant through a small opening without making the job almost impossible. If you don't maneuver well around little things, such as bottle mouths, pick a glass candy jar/canister, or a goldfish bowl, or a plastic box with a lid. Anything goes — so long as it isn't permanently encrusted with nasty chemicals. If the container you choose doesn't come with a lid, have a piece of glass cut that will cover the opening. You should be able to prop the glass lid up a bit. Or you can buy corks of various sizes at a hardware store.

Terrariums of modern times (the always-early Chinese had done it hundreds of years before) were invented in the 1840s by Nathaniel Ward, an English doctor/naturalist. They are often called Wardian cases. Dr. Ward was a real expert and managed to keep a case of ferns alive for eighteen years without ever adding water. Don't count on being able to do that.

Gardens-under-glass have become popular again in recent years. You can even buy kits containing everything needed to build a terrarium. Some kits come with plants, some don't. If you don't want to create your own planting tools, you may find it advisable to invest in at least a set of terrarium tools.

In essence, a terrarium is a small, enclosed, self-controlled world. It works because two important closed cycles are occurring in and around the plants.

In the moisture cycle, water from the soil and the leaves (which transpire, or give off water) evaporates. It then condenses on the glass, drops back into the soil, and is used again. The humidity stays high above the level you can achieve in your apartment. If your terrarium is balanced properly, don't expect to see the condensation during the day except perhaps right near soil level. Condensation usually happens at night when the temperature drops.

The second cycle is the oxygen cycle. Plants, like people, respire. They take in oxygen, use it in burning food for energy, and release carbon dioxide as a product of food burning. The carbon dioxide released is available for the plant to use, with light and water, in photosynthesis to produce food in the form of sugars. Oxygen is given off in the process of sugar formation. The oxygen is then used in respiration . . . and so on.

All you have to contribute to the cycles is enough — but not too much — water.

PICKING PLANTS FOR A TERRARIUM

Vital: pick plants that require the same conditions. That sounds very elementary, I know, but it's amazing how many terrariums go bad because the plants don't get along. If you put a small pittosporum in with a fern and water for the needs of the fern, the pittosporum is going to have the overwater droops. An even more exaggerated example is sedum with baby's tears. You must also match light requirements and temperature preferences.

Choose plants of different sizes — low, medium, and tall, relative, of course, to the size of the container you've selected. Plants in nature are certainly not all the same height. Why should they be in your terrarium? It's boring.

Choose, too, a variety of leaf shapes and markings. If you use a tinted glass container (which should be only lightly tinted, or not enough light will get in), choose plants that would live in shade in their native habitat. Use plants with bold markings that show through the tinted glass.

Don't mix greenhouse specimens with those you've dug out of the woods. There are apt to be bugs and diseases on plants brought in from outside that will go on the rampage among tender greenhouse-grown plants.

Another point: be sure that any plant you pick will actually go into the container. If you have to crush the roots or leaves to get it there, you start out with unhappy, mangled plants. Make a circle of your thumb and a finger — the size of the container opening — around the base of the plant you like. Raise your hand gently up the plant. If the leaves go smoothly through your fingers, the plant will safely go into your bottle. Remember the caution word "gently": if you break a plant, you'll probably have to buy it.

Some flowering plants, particularly African violets, do beautifully in terrariums. But I just can't recommend that you put them in narrow-mouthed bottles. Your conversation piece would soon disappear under a layer of dead flowers and pruned leaves (I'm assuming you would prune the leaves in order to achieve more flowers). So use goldfish bowls or other relatively open containers for flowering plants.

Go through "The Plant Guide" and check the requirements for each of the plants you'd like to include in a terrarium. The plants that are designated "terrarium" make up a basic list. Feel free to experiment once you have the planting and maintenance techniques down pat.

Consider special themes, such as:

A fern garden — using small specimens of different heights. You may have better luck with ferns in a terrarium than you do treating them as regular house plants.

A tropical garden — with a fern or two, *Episcia* (flame violet, usually grown for its pretty foliage), a small philodendron, *Saxifraga sarmentosa* (strawberry geranium), a tiny tidbit of baby's tears (*Helxine soleirolii*) but be careful, it grows like mad — perhaps a peperomia, and a little fittonia. All that is too much for an average-sized terrarium, so pick and choose.

A desert garden — this is the place to use your cacti and succulents, which can't be mixed with other plants. Be sure the mouth of the bottle is big enough to get the stuffed-shirt, unbending cacti in. Mix equal parts sand and soil to spread over the charcoal. Be generous with space. Don't cover the bottle because the plants rot in high humidity. Water very rarely. And watch out for prickles when handling the creatures.

Use your own imagination, within the limits imposed by the plants themselves. A sensibly designed and maintained terrarium should be a joy for several years.

Things you need:
  An attractive container
  Potting soil

BUILDING A TERRARIUM

Small pebbles or crushed pot for drainage
Charcoal
Heavy paper or kitchen funnel
Pickup tool (or grabber) — available at auto and hardware shops; or, if you're handy with chopsticks, try them.
A dowel or flat-ended stick for tamping
A selection of plants
Willingness to do it till you get it right

Plan your terrarium before you start construction. Draw a map of where you want each plant to be. Decide where to put stones, hills and valleys, the bits of driftwood you've been saving, or, if you lean that way, elves and pixies.

The preparation is basically the same for all terrariums. The amount of material you need will, of course, be different for different sizes of container.

Clean the container thoroughly, either by running it through a dishwasher or by washing it in hot, soapy water. Be sure to get every last driblet of soap out. If you need to clean stubborn stains with Windex or ammonia, let the container sit for several days to let the nasty fumes dissipate.

If a bottle is used, make a cone out of heavy paper or foil. It should be long enough and narrow enough to get almost to the bottom of the bottle so that dust and dirt won't spatter the sides. A kitchen funnel will do if it's long enough.

Drop drainage material into the bottle. Use a dowel or other tamper to spread it out evenly. The drainage layer should be about three-quarters of an inch deep, enough to collect excess water.

Add a thin (about a quarter of an inch) layer of crushed charcoal to just cover the drainage material. You should be able to direct the funnel enough to spread the charcoal evenly around. You can get charcoal at a nursery or pet shop. It absorbs odors and some excess moisture and keeps the soil from molding, which rots the plants.

You can mix the charcoal with the soil if you

want because the drainage layer will handle over-zealous watering. But If you don't use a separate drainage layer (which some people don't), the charcoal must be on the bottom so that it can do a drainage job, too.

Be sure that the soil you use is damp, so that it clings to itself without being sticky clumpy. Carefully drop soil through the funnel to the depth needed. A large bottle (which generally uses larger plants) should have a deeper soil layer than a small bottle. Regardless of size, however, you need at least two inches of soil. The total depth of all the materials put in, including soil, should be about one-fourth the depth of the container.

Now contour your land. You can't do it later, after the plants are put in place. The bigger the bottle, the more hills, valleys, or slopes you can build, but even the smallest container should at least slope from back to front.

Tamp all the soil down fairly firmly as you would in a pot. Add your pretty stones, shells, or driftwood bits, tamping them, too, into place so they won't run around.

How many plants you use depends on the size of the container. A small one — two quarts or less — can support one plant plus a little ground cover — which isn't necessary if you like the color of soil. I have a small round container holding just one beautiful miniature rose plus a few colorful pebbles scattered over a topping of chopped peat. You can figure approximately one plant per three-quarters gallon of space (for example, a five-gallon bottle should be able to handle seven or eight small plants). A tall, thin bottle, however, just won't handle more than a tall, thin plant plus some ground cover.

Don't crowd your plants. They need air around them and room to grow. If your main plant depends on leaf spread for its beauty, you won't want much around it (also, you would use a bowl-shaped container rather than one with straight sides). Leaves should not be allowed to touch the glass; they bruise too easily.

Dig a hole in the soil about two inches deep at the point where you want your main plant to live. Remove the plant carefully from its nursery pot by tapping the side of the pot on a firm surface. Gently brush the excess soil from the roots. A small soil ball should cling to the roots. Grasp the plant gently with the grabber tool. (If you don't feel comfortable handling tools, I suggest you practice first with objects that won't complain of mishandling.)

Maneuver the plant, roots first, through the bottle mouth so that the leaves go in smoothly. Stand the plant in its hole and tamp soil around it. If you can get two tools through the mouth, hold the plant in place with one while tamping with the other. If you can't, you may need several attempts to get the plant standing strongly in place. Patience.

I know a commercial terrarium builder who wraps each plant in a funnel of waxed paper for insertion into the container. It slides easily, unwraps itself, and can be withdrawn with the grabber.

Put the other plants in position the same as you did the first, tallest first, smallest last.

If the arrangement doesn't look the way you imagined it, rearrange as you work. Just don't wear the plants — and yourself — out.

Now comes the critical part. DO NOT OVER-WATER. Use only about one-fourth of a cup in a small container and about half a cup in a large one. To be really safe, use distilled water (NOT softened water) in the terrarium. The additives in tap water have no way to escape if they accumulate. But if your local water supply isn't too minerally, go ahead and use it after letting it sit a while for gases to escape.

Water with the mist sprayer you normally cheer on your house plants with. The spray distributes the measured water evenly. The soil should slowly change color as you spray. Enough water should go down the sides of the container to wash off spattered dirt. You can also water with a long-spouted watering can (only the measured amount, please) or a kitchen bulb-type baster.

To close or not to close? The original idea of terrariums called for their being sealed, creating a miniature habitat in which all elements were fully recycled. But terrarium balance is a delicate thing, and plants do like some fresh air. Completely sealed terrariums tend to overheat. Sealing terrariums is actually done more for the pride of the builder than for the benefit of the plants.

The safest practice is to water lightly and leave the lid off for a few hours so that excess water vapor escapes. Then replace the lid, preferably set slightly away from the mouth so that a little fresh air gets in. Moisture will still condense on the glass, creating a teeny tiny rain.

When you have your terrarium planted and watered just right, move it to a fairly shady place. It should remain there about a week while the plants recover from shock. Only then move it to the location you have selected (which, of course, determined the plants you used). A terrarium should never be in direct sun.

MAINTAINING THE TERRARIUM

Your terrarium should not need more water for a couple of months if it is small-mouthed and not much moisture escapes. A small bottle will need to be rewatered more often than a large one just because it doesn't hold much water. One of the simplest ways of knowing when it is time to rewater is to wait until you notice a slight droop in the plant leaves. Then don't be too, too sparing with the water. Like plants in pots, the terrarium plants must be watered enough for water to reach the roots. A few drops won't do it, but a tablespoonful might. The smaller the opening, the less water you should give. A brief spraying might be enough.

If you don't want to wait until leaves droop, watch the soil carefully. Discover how it looks when it's dry. If you can get your hand in the container, test the soil with your finger, as you would a potted plant.

You'll know quickly enough if you overwater. The glass fogs up very rapidly. Keep the cover off. If the fog doesn't go away, attach a small bit of sponge or paper towel to a dowel and press it into the soil. When it fills with water, bring it up, and wring it out. Keep repeating the sponge work until no more water collects in it.

Be sure to keep a watchful eye on your plants. If a leaf dies, gently cut it off with a razor blade or artist's knife attached to a stick. Draw the leaf out with the grabber. Prune overactive plants the same way. If they are too overactive, you may need to replace them with slower growers. When taking a plant out of a small-mouthed bottle, turn it (the plant, not the bottle) upside down — roots first — so leaves don't break off inside the bottle.

Check that the enclosed plants are getting the proper light. Turn the bottle occasionally so the plants don't acquire a leaning. If you don't get much light in your apartment in winter, you may want to put the terrarium under electric lights.

It is almost impossible to imagine that you will ever need to fertilize your terrarium. There is plenty of nutrient in the soil for the small amount of growing the plants should do. Also, there's a good chance that the fertilizer will actually burn the plants because there's no escape for excess as there is in a draining pot.

Probably ninety percent of terrariums that go bad do so from mold. It shows as a gray, dry "scum" on the soil. When you first spot mold, remove the soil it is attached to and you may be able to avoid its full effects. You may also be able to catch it in time by spraying the plants with a very mild fungicide. Check with your local garden store.

If you don't catch the mold and it takes over

completely, empty out the whole terrarium, wash the bottle thoroughly, and start all over again with new materials and a resolution to water with more care.

You can plant a bottle so that it lies on its side if you have a rack that holds it in position. You will need relatively more material for planting because of the larger surface to be covered, but, in return, you can use more plants. Be sure the soil can't run out of the mouth. You'll have to develop special tools for working sideways.

Plants should not be allowed to grow out the mouth of either an upright or prone container. If they do, you have to deal with two different environments. The leaves out in the open release more moisture than you dare replace by watering the soil in the terrarium.

Terrariums, when defined purely as environments that retain moisture, are very useful for your regular apartment plants. When you enclose a pot containing a rooting leaf or stem in a plastic bag, you are making a temporary terrarium. Turn a bottle or glass over a sick plant, and you make a terrarium sickroom. The forced raising of available moisture in the air does wonders for almost any plant.

PLASTIC PLANTS MAKE
PLASTIC IDEAS

MANY NEW OFFICE BUILDINGS FEATURE in their lobby and corridor decor vast planters of greenery. With luck and a good maintenance superintendent, they stay fresh and inviting, seeming to imply that humanitarian goals rather than greed motivate the work of the building's occupants.

However, in line with the trend toward simplified caretaking, the plants, on close inspection, often turn out to be plastic. The discovery that the greenery doesn't live, breathe, and grow may lead to the disappointing suspicion that perhaps neither do the occupants and their work.

You can do something to cancel that suspicion in your own small corner of the business world.

Remember the scene in Billy Wilder's film *The Apartment* where Jack Lemmon is working (late at night because he can't go home) in a large office filled with row upon row of identical desks? Every independent person's personal nightmare. Think how different the place would have looked if even a few desks had held large, green living plants.

Many of the plants that are suitable for apartment living will adjust equally well to an office environment, unless it's an office where the heat is turned off completely on winter nights and weekends.

What you generally have in offices, of course, is lots of fluorescent lights. You may not like them, but your plants will. So even if you're enclosed in a square, windowless box each day, you can share the box with a free-flowing philodendron, an insouciant syngonium, or a dramatic dracaena. You'll find it relaxing to share your problems with a plant. And in the midst of a snit about staff or supervisors, you can work the sprayer as a socially acceptable substitute for throwing ashtrays or books or secretaries. Make your frustrations constructive.

You must choose plants for closed boxes of offices very carefully. They should be able to stand long nights and dark weekends. Look in "The Plant Guide" for plants designated "office" which, under "Light," are suitable for any light. They will accept light even dimmer than north windows. *Aspidistra, Philodendron oxycardium*, and *Monstera* are among them. *Dieffenbachia* will work if it can have occasional holidays in a colleague's brighter office. Be sure, however, to transport the plant to brightness gradually to avoid shock.

In a dark office you must take special care that the plants get all the light they can. Don't turn your lights off when you go out for a long lunch. If you'll be away for a day, see that your secretary or a friend turns your office lights on. Be very sure that people who volunteer to water your plants know enough to check the soil first and to make sure the plants don't sit in pools of excess water. Plants receiving little light need little water because the activity of the leaves is almost nil.

The safest treatment you can give plants in a closed office is to keep them under a desk lamp or other light that you can attach to a timer. No plant really tolerates for long sitting in darkness at least two out of every seven days. Make sure that your building's weekend watchman knows about the lights. It would be very sad to lose your confidential aspidistra to an overzealous light-turner-outer.

Consider turning one or two shelves in your bookcase into an artificial light garden. Follow the

directions in "Artificial Light to Help the Sun."
You can, then, have flowering plants in your office
that will soothe your spirit, impress visitors, and
give you a good excuse for delaying the work
you're trying to avoid, if only for the length of
time it takes to remove dead flower heads, spray
the leaves, check the water in the pebble tray, or
pinch off overenthusiastic growing tips. The latter
can be an exercise in beheading that will get you
in less trouble than if you tried it with people.

If your office has that glory of glories, a window, you and your plants are sitting pretty, especially if they face south, east, or west. Make certain, however, that you thoroughly recognize and
understand your own behavior. If you just like
some greenery nearby, stick to the plants called
"office." They are all fairly rugged and can with-
stand the occasional days in which you are unwill-
ing or unable to heed them. As in your own apartment, be sure that plants in south-facing windows
have some shielding from summer sun. You may
be the center of your universe at work during the
week, but your absence on weekends doesn't prevent the sun from coming up.

Those bright windows can profitably be used as
growing places for cacti and other succulent plants.
They will not only endure but will downright enjoy waterless and non-air-conditioned weekends,
within limits, of course; if they need watering on
Friday, they'll be in even worse shape by Monday.

Weekends — the hostile times — can be down-
played for humidity-loving plants by growing the
plants in a terrarium (see "Terrariums"). Choose
the plants, of course, according to the location you
can allot to the terrarium. Plants under glass in
your office have the advantage of being protected
from indiscriminately tossed papers. The hurly-
burly of office activity need not disturb them, but
they are still there to act as a sounding board for
your great ideas and plans.

In whatever kind of office you spend each day,

there are factors you must consider just as you would in your apartment.

Where is the blower that provides heat in winter and cooled air in summer? Locate the draft-free places for your plants' homes.

Is all heat turned off over winter weekends? No indoor-adjusted plant will survive for more than a few weeks a regular drop to forty degrees followed by a quick Monday-morning rise into the seventies.

Is the water supply two floors away, making it easy for you to decide to put off watering your plants until another day? Forget growing plants. They don't need your negligence along with the commotion of office life.

Does your water cooler or fountain give really cold water? Always let the water you have drawn (as though you went to the well) for your plants warm to room temperature before watering them.

Is the air so dry as to make papers cling to each other or sparks fly between you and the metal equipment? Take extra care that the pebble tray is always well filled and that your sprayer is as close as your telephone.

If you can serve your office plants well, they will serve you well. A complete review of the ecology of your office will show you what conditions prevail. Pick plants that are suitable to the conditions you perceive. Care for them as a regular activity of your office day. The freshness that healthy plants can bring to stale thoughts can be as important as a properly organized filing cabinet.

APARTMENT PLANT CHART

FOLIAGE: plant grown for its leaves ⎫
FLOWERING: plant grown for its flowers ⎬ many plants are both
                                  ⎭
EASY: minimal care needed
TERRARIUM: plant small and grows relatively slowly
OFFICE: plant is hardy and will grow under fluorescent light
WATER: plant will grow in water instead of soil
HANGING AND CLIMBING: can be displayed

PLANT	FOLIAGE	FLOWERING	EASY	TERRARIUM	OFFICE	WATER	HANGING	CLIMBING	LIGHT REQUIREMENTS*
Adiantum	✔			✔					E W (N)
Aechmea	✔	✔		✔ (when small)					any†
Aglaonema	✔		✔	✔	✔	✔			any†
Anthurium	✔	✔		✔					E W (S)
Araucaria	✔ (tree)								N E W
Asparagus	✔			✔			✔	✔	E W (N)
Aspidistra	✔		✔		✔				any‡
Asplenium	✔			✔					E W (N)
Begonia	✔	✔		✔			✔		E W (S)
Billbergia	✔	✔	✔						E W S
Cactus	✔	✔		✔					S
Ceropegia	✔	✔		✔			✔		any†
Chlorophytum	✔		✔				✔		E W (S)
Cissus	✔		✔				✔	✔	any†
Citrus	✔	✔							S
Clivia	✔	✔	✔						any†
Codiaeum	✔			✔					S
Coleus	✔	✔	✔	✔		✔			E W S
Columnea	✔	✔		✔			✔		E W S
Cordyline	✔					✔			E W

* Light requirement in parentheses means special conditions apply. See "Light" under corresponding plant in Chapter "The Plant Guide."
† Any light direction with the exception of extremes.
‡ Plant will accept even dark corners.

PLANT	FOLIAGE	FLOWERING	EASY	TERRARIUM	OFFICE	WATER	HANGING	CLIMBING	LIGHT REQUIREMENTS*
Crassula	✓			✓					E W (N)
Crossandra	✓	✓		✓					E W
Cyperus	✓		✓			✓			any†
Davallia	✓			✓			✓		E W (N)
Dieffenbachia	✓		✓		✓	✓			any‡
Dizygotheca	✓			✓					E W
Dracaena	✓		✓	✓	✓	✓			any†
Episcia	✓	✓		✓			✓		E W
Euphorbia	✓	✓	✓						E W
Fatshedera	✓		✓		✓	✓		✓	E W N
Ficus	✓		✓		✓		✓	✓	any†
Fittonia	✓			✓					any†
Hedera	✓		✓			✓	✓	✓	any†
Helxine	✓		✓	✓					N
Howea	✓				✓				E W
Hoya	✓	✓	✓				✓	✓	E W (S)
Impatiens	✓	✓	✓						E W (S)
Maranta	✓		✓	✓					E W N
Monstera	✓		✓		✓			✓	any†
Neomarica	✓	✓	✓						any†
Nephrolepis	✓			✓			✓		E W (N S)
Pandanus	✓		✓	✓	✓				N E W
Pelargonium	✓	✓					✓		E W (S)
Pellionia	✓			✓			✓		E W (S N)
Peperomia	✓		✓	✓					E W (N)
Philodendron	✓		✓	✓	✓	✓	✓	✓	any†
Pilea	✓			✓					E W
Pittosporum	✓			✓ (when small)					E W (S)

* Light requirement in parentheses means special conditions apply. See "Light" under corresponding plant in Chapter "The Plant Guide."
† Any light direction with the exception of extremes.
‡ Plant will accept even dark corners.

PLANT	FOLIAGE	FLOWERING	EASY	TERRARIUM	OFFICE	WATER	HANGING	CLIMBING	LIGHT REQUIREMENTS*
Plectranthus	✔	✔				✔	✔		E W (S)
Pteris	✔			✔					any†
Rhoeo	✔	✔	✔						any†
Rosa		✔		✔					E W (S)
Saintpaulia		✔		✔					E W (S)
Sansevieria	✔		✔		✔				any‡
Saxifraga	✔	✔	✔	✔			✔		E W (S)
Schefflera	✔				✔	✔			any†
Scindapsis	✔		✔	✔		✔	✔	✔	any†
Sedum	✔		✔	✔					S
Spathiphyllum	✔	✔	✔						any†
Syngonium	✔		✔		✔	✔	✔	✔	E W N
Tolmiea	✔		✔				✔		E W N
Tradescantia	✔		✔			✔	✔		any†

* Light requirement in parentheses means special conditions apply. See "Light" under corresponding plant in Chapter "The Plant Guide."
† Any light direction with the exception of extremes.
‡ Plant will accept even dark corners.

GLOSSARY

ANTHER: the knoblike top of a stamen (the long, thin male sexual organ) in a flower. Anthers bear pollen and are often yellow or golden in color.

BRACT: a leaf-shaped plant structure associated with, and often looking like part of, the flower. The red "flowers" on *Euphorbia* are actually bracts.

BROMELIAD: any member of the bromeliad, or pineapple, family. In general, they have thick, saw-edged leaves that grow in rosettes adapted to collecting water, thus eliminating the need for extensive roots in deep soil. *Aechmea* and *Billbergia* are among bromeliads commonly grown indoors.

CALLUS: a thickened and hardened mass of cells that develops over a wound or cut in plant tissue. A callus must grow on a cutting end in order for roots to develop.

DORMANCY: a period of stopped or slowed growth.

EPIPHYTE: a plant adapted to having its roots exposed to air; often called an air plant. The roots serve mainly as an anchor; the leaves handle the bulk of the water- and food-absorbing function. Most bromeliads are epiphytes.

FROND: a leaf on a fern or palm. Fronds are usually divided into many smaller leaflets which resemble true leaves.

GENUS: (plural: *genera*) see Species.

OFFSET: a very short runner that grows at the side of the base of some plants such as *Clivia* and *Sansevieria*. It may develop roots of its own and can be separated from the mother plant.

PHOTOSYNTHESIS: the complex process by which plant cells containing a substance called chlorophyll convert inorganic carbon dioxide and water into organic carbohydrates under the influence of sunlight. Photosynthesis is the basic process from which all life, both plant and animal, is derived.

PLANTLET: a little leaf and stem structure usually growing at the end of a runner. It resembles a miniature version of the mother plant except for lack of roots, which easily develop if the plantlet is allowed to rest in a rooting medium. *Saxifraga* and *Episcia* are among plants producing plantlets.

RHIZOME: a specialized stem that grows horizontally, usually underground, and produces both regular stems and roots. Certain begonias and ferns develop rhizomes.

RUNNER: a long stem that grows horizontally from some plants with a small plantlet at its end. If in contact with soil, the plantlet may develop roots of its own, thus spreading and propagating new plants. *Chlorophytum* and *Episcia* are among plants that develop runners.

SPATHE: a bract cupping or often forming a base for a spike bearing small flowers, as in the *Anthurium* or the *Spathiphyllum*.

SPECIES: a kind of plant, usually defined scientifically as one which interbreeds freely with others of its type. Several different species with only minor differences among them are grouped in a *genus* (plural: *genera*). The full botanical name of any plant is made up of genus followed by species, for example: *Philodendron oxycardium* or *Philodendron hastatum*.

SPORES: tiny particles found in brown cases on the backs of fern fronds. Unlike the seeds of less primitive plants, they are asexual, but when planted, they grow into sexual structures called prothalli. These, in turn, are fertilized and produce a new asexual fern, the one recognizable as a house plant. This two-stage reproduction method is called alternation of generations.

STOMATA: (singular: *stoma*) tiny openings in leaves through which gases enter and leave and through which water is given off in transpiration. Stomata must be able to open and close freely, thus the need for keeping leaves clean.

SUCCULENT: a plant with leaves and/or stems modified to store water against the dry periods in its native habitat. The extreme examples are the cacti whose leaves become spines and whose stems serve as rounded storage "barrels." Lesser degrees of succulence are found in many plants.

TRANSPIRATION: the loss of water from a leaf by evaporation. This is a normal process but can be harmful if the air around the leaf is dry, encouraging too rapid evaporation. Most plants are healthier if the air is humid, slowing transpiration.

VARIETY: a subdivision of a species, which can occur spontaneously in nature or through selective breeding of plants. That a plant is a variety instead of a separate species is indicated by a third part to its botanical name, for example: *Dracaena fragrans massangeana* or *Dracaena godseffiana* "Florida Beauty."

PLANT INDEX AND COMMON-NAME GUIDE

Note that all page references will be found at the botanical name of the plant, even though the common name may be used in the text. For ease of use, all common names of apartment plants are cross-referenced to their botanical names. A page number in *italic* type indicates that an illustration will be found on that page.

Adiantum, 34–35
  tererum, 34
Aechmea, 35–37
  fasciata, 35
  racinae, 37
African evergreen. See *Syngonium*
African violet. See *Saintpaulia ionantha*
Aglaonema, 37–38, 160
  commutatum, 37
airplane plant. See *Chlorophytum*
aluminum plant. See *Pilea cadierei*
American wonder lemon. See *Citrus limonia ponderosa*
angel wing begonia. See *Begonia corallina*
Anthurium, 38–39
  scherzerianum, 38
apostle plant. See *Neomarica*
aralia. See *Dizygotheca elegantissima*
Araucaria excelsa, 39–40
arrowroot. See *Maranta arundinacea*
artillery plant. See *Pilea microphylla*
asparagus fern. See *Asparagus plumosus*
Asparagus plumosus, 40–42
  sprengeri, 40, 41, 42
Aspidistra elatior, 7, 42–43, 86, 144, 175
  lurida. See *Aspidistra elatior*
Asplenium nidus, 19, 43–44
Australian bracken. See *Pteris tremula*
Australian umbrella tree. See *Schefflera actinophylla*

baby's tears. See *Helxine soleirolii*
ball fern. See *Davallia*
banjo fig. See *Ficus lyrata*
beefsteak begonia. See *Begonia feasti*
Begonia, 44–48, 129, 150, 155
  argenteo-guttata, 45

  corallina, 47
  feasti, 46
  masoniana, 46
  rex, 19, 46–47, 131
  rhizomatous, 44, 46, 132
  semperflorens, 47
  serratipetala, 45
  tuberous, 47
Billbergia nutans, 36, 48
bird's nest fern. See *Asplenium nidus*
boat lily. See *Rhoeo spathacea*
Boston fern. See *Nephrolepis exaltata*
bracken fern. See *Pteris*
brake fern. See *Pteris*
Brassaia. See *Schefflera actinophylla*
bromeliad, 19, 36, 132
burro's tail. See *Sedum morganianum*
busy Lizzie. See *Impatiens sultanii*

Cactus, 7, 19, 48–50, 123, 167, 176. See also *Opuntia*
Calathea, 83
cast-iron plant. See *Aspidistra elatior*
Cephalocereus, 49
Cereus peruviana, 49
Ceropegia woodii, 51, 155
Chinese evergreen. See *Aglaonema*
Chlorophytum elatum, 52, 132, 155
  bicheti, 52
Cissus, 53–54, 124, 157
  antarctica, 53–54
  rhombifolia, 8, 53–54
Citrus, 54–55, 122
  aurantifolia, 54–55
  limonia ponderosa, 54–55
  mitis, 54
  taitensis, 54–55

climbing aralia, 71
Clivia miniata, 55, 56, 57, 123, 132
Codiaeum variegatum, 57–58, 159
  aucubaevolium, 57
Coleus blumei, 58, 153
Columnea microphylla, 59, 155
Common philodendron. See *Philodendron
  oxycardium*
Cordyline marginata. See *Dracaena marginata
  terminalis*, 60
corn plant. See *Dracaena fragrans*
Costa Rican plant. See *Columnea microphylla*
Crassula argentea, 60–61, 131
  arborescens, 61
creeping fig. See *Ficus pumila*
Crossandra infundibuliformis, 61–62
croton. See *Codiaeum variegatum*
crown of thorns. See *Euphorbia splendens*
Cyperus alternifolius, 62–63, 120, 133, 159

Davallia, 63–64, 132
  mariesii, 64
deer-foot fern. See *Davallia*
devil's ivy. See *Scindapsus*
Dieffenbachia, 64–65, 134, 175
  maculata, 64
Dizygotheca elegantissima, 65–66
Dracaena, 65–68, 124, 134
  deremensis warnecki. See *Dracaena
    warneckii*
  fragrans, 66–68
    massangeana, 67, 68
  godseffiana, 66, 67, 68
  marginalis, 66, 67, 68
  terminalis. See *Cordyline terminalis*
  warneckii, 66–88
dumb cane. See *Dieffenbachia*

elephant's ear. See *Philodendron hastatum*
emerald feather. See *Asparagus sprengeri*
emerald ripple. See *Peperomia caperata*
English baby's tears, 78
English ivy. See *Hedera helix*
Epiphyllum, 50
Episcia, 19, 69–70, 122, 132, 134, 146, 155, 167
  cupreata, 69
Euphorbia splendens, 70–71, 123
  bojeri, 70

false aralia. See *Dizygotheca elegantissima*
false arrowroot. See *Maranta leuconeura*
fan iris. See *Neomarica*
fan palm. See *Howea*
Fatshedera lizei, 71–72
Fatsia japonica, 71

fern, 19, 117, 133, 141, 146, 155, 166, 167. See
  also *Adiantum; Asparagus, plumosus;
  Asparagus sprengeri; Asplenium nidus;
  Davallia; Nephrolepis exaltata; Pteris*
Ficus, 72–75, 157
  benjamina, 72, 73, 74
  elastica, 72, 73, 74, 126, 134
  lyrata, 72, 74
  pandurata. See *Ficus lyrata*
  pumila, 72, 73, 74, 75, 129
  repens. See *Ficus pumila*
fiddleleaf fig. See *Ficus lyrata*
fiddleleaf philodendron. See *Philodendron
  bipennifolium*
finger aralia. See *Dizygotheca elegantissima*
firecracker flower. See *Crossandra
  infundibuliformis*
Fittonia, 75–76, 157, 167
  argyroneura, 75–76
  verschaffeltii, 76
flame nettle. See *Coleus blumei*
flame violet. See *Episcia*
flamingo flower. See *Anthurium*
Florida Beauty. See *Dracaena godseffiana*
Fluffy Ruffles. See *Nephrolepis*
Foster's Favorite. See *Aechmea*
friendship plant. See *Pilea involucrata*

geranium. See *Pelargonium*
glacier ivy, 77
gold-dust plant. See *Dracaena godseffiana*
goldfish flower. See *Columnea microphylla*
grape ivy. See *Cissus rhombifolia*

heartleaf. See *Philodendron oxycardium*
hearts entangled. See *Ceropegia woodii*
Hedera helix, 71, 76–77, 124, 142, 153, 157,
  159
Helxine soleirolii, 78, 166, 167
Howea, 79, 141
  belmoreana, 79
  fosteriana, 79
Hoya carnosa, 80–81, 123, 124, 155

Impatiens sultanii, 81–82, 124, 129, 157
India rubber plant. See *Ficus elastica*
Indian fig. See *Ficus benjamina*
Irish moss. See *Helxine soleirolii*
iron cross begonia. See *Begonia masoniana*
ivy. See *Cissus; Hedera helix; Plectranthus*
ivy-leaved geranium. See *Pelargonium
  peltatum*

Jacob's coat. See *Coleus blumei*
jade plant. See *Crassula argentea*

Plant Index and Common-Name Guide   185

scent-leaved geranium. See *Pellargonium crispum, denticulatum, graveolens, tomentosum*

Schefflera actinophylla, 104–105

screwpine. See *Pandanus*

Scindapsus, 105–106
  aureus, 106

Sedum, 107, 131, 166
  adolphi, 107
  morganianum, 107, 155

snake plant. See *Sansevieria*

spathe flower. See *Spathiphyllum*

Spathiphyllum, 38, 108–109, 117, 133
  cannaefolium, 108
  clevelandii, 108

spider plant. See *Chlorophytum elatum*

spleenwort. See *Asplenium nidus*

split-leaf philodendron. See *Monstera deliciosa*

stonecrop. See *Sedum*

strawberry begonia. See *Saxifraga sarmentosa*

strawberry geranium. See *Saxifraga sarmentosa*

string of hearts. See *Ceropegia woodii*

Swedish ivy. See *Plectranthus australis*

sweetheart vine. See *Philodendron oxycardium*

Swiss cheese plant. See *Monstera deliciosa*

sword fern. See *Nephrolepis exaltata*

Syngonium, 109–110, 144, 159, 160
  podophyllum, 109

table fern. See *Pteris*

tailflower. See *Anthurium*

threadleaf. See *Dizygotheca elegantissima*

Ti plant. See *Cordyline terminalis*

Tolmiea menziesii, 33, 110–111, 155

Tradescantia fluminensis, 111–112, 124, 129, 157, 159

tree ivy. See *Fatshedera lizei*

twelve apostles. See *Neomarica*

umbrella plant. See *Cyperus alternifolius*

walking anthericum. See *Chlorophytum*

wandering Jew. See *Tradescantia fluminensis*

watermelon begonia. See *Peperomia sandersii*

watermelon peperomia. See *Peperomia sandersii*

wax begonia. See *Begonia semperflorens*

wax plant. See *Hoya carnosa*

weeping fig. See *Ficus benjamina*

window-leaf philodendron. See *Monstera deliciosa*

Zebrina pendula. See *Tradescantia fluminensis*